Many Windows

SEASONS OF THE HEART

BOOKS BY FAITH BALDWIN

Three Women
Departing Wings
Alimony
The Office-Wife
The Incredible Year
Make-Believe
Today's Virtue
Skyscraper
Week-end Marriage
District Nurse
Self-made Woman
Beauty
White-Collar Girl
Love's a Puzzle
Innocent Bystander
Wife versus Secretary
Within a Year
Honor Bound
American Family
The Puritan Strain
The Moon's Our Home
Private Duty
The Girls of Divine Corners
Men Are Such Fools!
That Man Is Mine
The Heart Has Wings
Twenty-four Hours a Day
Manhattan Nights
Enchanted Oasis
Rich Girl, Poor Girl
Hotel Hostess
The High Road

Career by Proxy
White Magic
Station Wagon Set
Rehearsal for Love
"Something Special"
Letty and the Law
Medical Center
And New Stars Burn
Temporary Address: Reno
The Heart Remembers
Blue Horizons
Breath of Life
Five Women in Three Novels
The Rest of My Life with You
Washington, U.S.A.
You Can't Escape
He Married A Doctor
Change of Heart
Arizona Star
A Job for Jenny
No Private Heaven
Woman on Her Way
Sleeping Beauty
Give Love the Air
Marry for Money
They Who Love
The Golden Shoestring
Look Out for Liza
The Whole Armor
The Juniper Tree
Face Toward the Spring
Many Windows

POETRY

Sign Posts

Widow's Walk

Many Windows

SEASONS OF THE HEART

Faith Baldwin

RINEHART & COMPANY, INC.

NEW YORK   TORONTO

Published simultaneously in Canada by
Clarke, Irwin & Company, Ltd., Toronto

*This book with love and gratitude is
dedicated to three from the East. . . .*

SRI ARBUNDIA, *whose teaching is spiritual
enlightenment;*

KWAN-YIN, *whose gift is quietude;
and*
HUNG-WU, *who said, "The house of life has
many windows."*

Foreword

THE MATERIAL HOUSE IN WHICH I LIVE HAS MANY WINDOWS and I have often thought, looking from one or the other, how, lifelong we look through windows: often with interest; sometimes with boredom or distaste; and when fortunate, with appreciation or anticipation.

Some are the windows of the houses, closed around us for shelter. Most of us have lived in more than one. But we also look through the windows of friend or stranger; through those of hotels, hospitals, trains and planes, and the round portholes of ships.

Often, we look from the outside, as we walk along road or street, idly, or with curiosity or envy. Looking in, from without, I have seen innumerable things: men and women quarrelling, once with violence; a child crowded against a pane, his face luminous; the contorted features of an older child, standing forlorn and weeping; a girl beating her fists against glass. I have seen a woman threaten suicide, witnessed people dancing, eating, reading, or listening to music. And often I have seen happiness and love in homes without tragedy and sin as I looked at lighted Christmas trees.

I do not know why the men and women quarrelled, or what one child awaited, or what caused the other's grief. I cannot guess what tensions flung the fists of a young girl against the glass, or what drove the woman toward the skull-and-crossbones bottle. That woman lived in back of me and, as I watched, too stunned to move, she threw the bottle into the kitchen sink and ran, crying, from the room. I heard her crying for a long time, for all windows were open to the hot city night.

How could I tell who were partnered in the dance, or know those who sat at card tables, or know what they ate, drank, read or heard; whose hands trimmed the trees?

At one time or another, all of us have waited by windows. Who will move on the street or path? Doctor, lawyer, messenger, lover? Sometimes we wait in fear or anguish, or expectation sharp as pain. Often, we wait too long, or not long enough. Yet always the expected moment must arrive, infused with fatality or happiness, relief or anxiety.

Through glass—which appears durable, but is susceptible to violence, falling before storm or intruder—we see much of our lives. When a window gives on beauty, we may reach past bud or flower, mountains or sea, in wonder. When it affords a glimpse of young lovers—or of older, more slowly walking—we may remember, each according to experience, fulfillment or frustration intensely personal, and so become conscious of more than the moving forms of strangers. Beyond these unknown people there is much: nostalgia, sorrow, happiness, or gratitude recalled in agony. Sometimes there is anticipation, and frequently, envy.

From an airplane, the miniature world is wide and often seeming empty, or there is no world beneath the clustered clouds. From train windows the traveller sees much, however briefly; but from any house the view is restricted.

We also are windows. From these windows of self we look out at people, and they look in at us. But we are so devised that we can never clearly be seen. For that which friend or stranger, lover or enemy, child or parent sees is obscure, a shape, an appearance, sometimes a distortion, differing for each in-looker.

On this winter day, when the windows of my work room are streaked with old rain, the ground covered with new snow, the sky the color of apathy, yet with blue beyond my vision, I am minded to look through some of the windows of the year. You have looked through many of these—or will. We have seen, we shall see, different things; yet basically the same.

Look with me.

Contents

[13]

Many Windows

SEASONS OF THE HEART

December

THERE ARE PEOPLE WHO, IN DECEMBER, FEEL FATIGUE, AS IF
the past months had suddenly descended upon them with
tangible weight; and they look toward January as the year's
beginning, when the weight will certainly and almost immediately be lifted.

But December is a year-beginning in itself, for toward
its conclusion there is Christmas, and who has not felt the
Beginning which is a symbol of that day has missed much.

Ten days, two weeks, before the bells ring out, we have
brought the big boxes from the attic and marvelled how
things, securely packed, tied and put away, can shatter. I
cannot believe that the field mouse which may somehow
have found shelter, or the moth which got in—heaven
knows how!—has untied string, removed paper and done the
damage. But every year there are things to be replaced, although our trees nowadays are not as enormous as the ones

we used to have. These I can trim myself, and have for the last few years; only the tipmost branches call for the kitchen stepladder upon which I am as unsteady as a small ship at sea. But I manage. I work with one hand, holding to a bookcase, or to the top of a heavy screen, with the other.

There is about this ritual a certain technique. First, I like to be alone, for these years differ from the ones in which we trimmed the tree on Christmas Eve so the children wouldn't see until morning. They differ, too, from many thereafter when all, or some of them, in jeans and pinafores, undertook the job themselves. Even in those days of the bigger house, the huge tree, and the room set aside for it, I had ceased to use the strings of lights, and I never liked dripping tinsel. Lights were fine, and could be seen as far away as the road, but there was always the business of someone having to crawl under the tree and turn them on. Besides, it is less of a fire hazard not to use them. So I don't. I rely at night upon the living-room lamps, which reflect on the colored globes and decorations, or by day upon the sunlight from the nearby windows.

I am devoted to angels. They fly all about the tree, and one, with downcast eyes and with yellow hair—made, I think, of feathers—stands at the top. Her face is pensive and not very pious. She has a stiff, fluted skirt and, being hollow, she fits on that last, highest, barest stem which was cropped to make the tree the proper height.

My friend John, going to Maine every year at Thanksgiving, returns with trees from his uncle's farm, for his family and mine. They are heeled-in and cared for until they can be set up indoors in a fastening-type container, and thereafter I crawl under mine daily to give it water.

The friend, who with his wife comes to us Christmas night, is sad because Christmas trees are cut down, made gay for a season, then tossed away. He needn't be. They serve many purposes. They help support those who grow them; they gladden the eyes of children and adults alike; and they come, as a rule, from places where they have innumerable kindred and where, if the grower is clever, another is planted for each one cut. Besides, we do not toss ours on an ash heap. We take it to a nearby field as shelter for birds in winter, and there, many months later, burn it properly, for the ascending smoke is sweet, the ashes clean and probably good for the soil. In this way the tree—having been married to the gaiety of the season, and the season having passed—commits a sort of suttee.

When I get ready to trim, I put the boxes on the floor and on the couch, sort the ornaments so each will be ready to occupy its proper place. I have no patience with "decorator" trees; they are all right for shop windows, but I don't like them stark white or all-over blue, or shocking pink or done up with cabbage roses. I like a happy hodgepodge of old and new, though I do endeavor to separate colors not compatible. I have a few flowery-looking ornaments, in pinks, but I keep them distant from the standard reds.

While I am trimming, I take my little radio and find a station which is broadcasting carols. Not too many give me all of my favorite carol, "Little Town of Bethlehem," but usually there is a mélange which is pleasant and fitting.

[19]

If it is cold outside, so much the better. And a white Christmas is like a frosted cake, except that in the country it would be more practical if the white stayed on the ground, but off the driveways, paths and roads; or on the housetops —although not enough of it to deter Santa if his reindeer are not equipped with snow tires.

Trimming, I find my feet hurt, so I kick off my shoes and continue in stockinged feet. This is soothing, but an error if I have reason to walk across the floor boards and not the rugs, for if there is anything, short of ice, more slippery than old waxed and polished floor boards, I don't know it. Of course, you usually don't skate on ice in nylons.

Generally, it takes me four hours or more to trim, sweep up what I've broken—I always break something— stand back, admire and criticize. Then there's a period in which I move things from one branch to another and think I haven't enough for the back of the tree (which no one sees).

Also I check the old things. There is a tiny saxophone, its red, blue and silver worn and rubbed. It is made of the same fragile material as the globes, and how it has survived so long I do not know. I once had a dozen Santa Claus balls, complete with whiskers; there were three left last year. Where is the silly bird cage, and how many birds in variegated colors have survived? The wooden things and some of the heavier glass have been with me over thirty years . . . although many now adorn the trees of adults who, as children, first saw them. Some years ago, a friend gave me a small flock of miniature redbirds made of wood; these are affixed to branches by pins and will last a long time.

People send packages from their homes or from shops, and the ribbons have enchanting little figures or bits of artificial holly, trees, or strings of tiny balls tied into them. These I keep for next year's tree. And I have a friend who makes her own Christmas cards of felt: one year a pale pink reindeer with tinsel at its throat, the next a little wreath. These go on the tree, too. Each year I forget, perhaps deliberately, what I have, and it is an excitement to rediscover the Christmas-decorated trinkets which were last year's package trimmings.

Angels fly over lintels here. Some, quite old, are felt dolls with absurd pretty boy and girl faces—but they have wings. One boy in a blue checked shirt and blue overalls has gingham wings to match his shirt.

In the entry hall is a small sleigh. I have saved a Santa Claus for it, but something has happened to his head; he will not hold it upright. I prop him up, however, and put tiny packages in with him, bits of anything wrapped in bright paper, and a small sack which I filched from one of the angels. There's a whip-holder socket, with a belled whip in it; and for a year or two Santa has been accompanied by a porcelain cherub orchestra from Italy, which stands beside the sleigh.

I have a crèche from Oberammergau, small, delicately carved; one of light wood under a bell of glass—and why that cracked in the attic I can't imagine. There is also a dark one upstairs with no glass; and another, bigger, on the mantel over the fireplace, flanked by a procession of carved wooden angels, each wearing a star-sprinkled, pastel-colored gown and carrying a tiny candle.

People like the way the house looks at Christmas, but none more than I.

Some things traditional at this time of year I have either never liked, or no longer enjoy. I have never liked plum pudding, for example (or wedding cake for that matter; no wonder you dream on it!), and after the first few years of listening to Lionel Barrymore, I grew tired of dear, horrible old Scrooge on radio. I used to like him, when my father read to me and I shivered with delicious terror, wept with sorrow for Tiny Tim, and cheered up enormously when all lived happily afterwards. By now the story has palled, and I can do without it.

Life has brought me a lot of Christmases—and not only on December twenty-fifth. I can remember a November day which seemed to me all Christmases rolled into one; and again, many years later, a June that bestowed more gifts than most Noels. . . . Indeed, all through the years there have been the unexpected gifts, material and spiritual, which made Christmas come alive no matter what the season. If your children, for instance, are born in March or July or April, are they not presents wrapped in blankets, smelling sweetly of baby oil and newness, and more marvellous than any jewel in a leather box, wrapped in silver and tied with gold?

What do I want for Christmas this year?

For the world, peace, which is the Christmas promise, but one that cannot be fulfilled unless we work for it as a reward. For all men, brotherhood, likewise implicit in the Christmas pledge, but also for us to achieve; for everyone, enough shelter, nourishment, a school, a church, and security. This, too, is a far goal.

I wish a return to decency. I do not mean censorship or the control by law of what we shall read and see, on stage or screen, by way of entertainment or education. There are many factors in living, once whispered about behind locked doors, but now revealed. And that is much the healthier way. Adult discussion of any valid problem is therapeutic and, if set in a strong narrative or acted in a good play, so much the better. But I am tired of all that is deliberately sensational, vapid, uninstructive and even harmful to those who are without intelligence or who are too young to evaluate.

All these bore me, and I haven't intentionally read a book of this type or seen such a play or motion picture for years.

But it is not new, this deliberate appeal to the baser instincts. Read the novels and plays of the Restoration if you don't believe me. Nor is it, as some think, indecent merely because it deals with sex. Shakespeare wrote of the physical realistically, with understanding and justice, but without scareheads. All things natural are to be respected and given their proper value, for without the elemental drives there would be no world at all. In every animal, on two

[23]

feet or four, in every bird and insect, and in all growth about us, there are the negative and the positive polarities—the female and the male.

Love is something else, but its fulfillment in the man and woman relationship recognizes sex as a component part, thereby informed with beauty.

The capitalization by clinical dissection of love or sex or both, separately or together, wearies me. It is fashionable to accept it, as it has, for a long time, been fashionable to unmask the psychological difficulties of earlier eras. The Puritans were people, too; and the Victorians were a lusty lot. It is commonly accepted that lack of understanding—the prudery of the drawn blind—made innumerable people and homes wretched and filled the asylums. But there is certainly a middle ground, neither all prudery nor all pornography!

The very serious—perhaps not-too-successful—writers find it imperative to dwell upon the evils of each era. This has been so since there were writers. Look at a translation from early Latin or Greek. Even then, authors declaimed, bemoaned and wrung their hands, but some also amused themselves, much as their successors do now, by classic obscenity. Every era, everywhere, has used the what-are-we-coming-to? theme, in all departments of violent, undisciplined life. Do you think there were no adulterous men and women before our time, or before the white man set foot upon Cape Cod? Have you forgotten Europe and Greece and Rome; Asia and Egypt and civilizations even older than they? Primitive tribes have rituals and tabus which seem astonishing to us and, always, the scandalous deviations from them. Do you believe that there were no thieves and no murderers until our day? Of course, you do not.

The time of Him Whose birth we celebrate this season was replete with murders, theft and adultery . . . and He was born only a brief two thousand years ago. He knew it. He was not, one supposes, happy in the knowing; but He said, "Neither do I condemn thee; go, and sin no more." And later spoke with compassion and promise to the thief, crucified beside Him.

All this we know, yet as I listen to people talk, as I read newspapers, watch movies and television, I wonder if people believe there have not been what we call "juvenile delinquents" before now? Certainly some of us are old enough to remember the wild packs of children, terrorizing as they wandered through Russia after the First World War; and look at those turned loose everywhere after the Second. We all remember those stories.

Now it has become fashionable to publicize the young delinquent and to explain him: he has had an inferior environment, or is from a broken home and is therefore exposed to any number of psychological factors which trigger him until the club falls, the shot is fired, or the switch blade is flashed. Exceptions in environment and circumstances only prove the rule, some say.

When I suggest that we should seek prevention rather than cure, all the many serious, informed agencies which are working just for this will agree with me.

[25]

But prevention is not always possible, for, while much depends on the discipline, not of an institution, but of a household which sets an example, even more depends on love. To this the well-informed will also agree. The question is how to teach people to love.

As for "example," it is not set by books, or by nasty little screen offerings, which exalt the adulterer, the thief, the murderer, no matter to what proper punishment he is brought, or whether wearing modern dress or tricked out in period costume. There is an ugly nakedness which cannot be clothed. In fiction, the highwayman, the robber, the bandit, can appear in fascinating historical detail or, as is also popular, he can wear well-tailored clothes and rise from rags to riches, though rarely by the Horatio Alger formula. In real life, he is often esteemed, received and envied, until, as sometimes happens, we find him behind steel bars. Once there, he is repudiated, excoriated and then forgotten by all except those who loved him. Sometimes, after a generation or two has passed away and he with it, he is, as it were, disinterred, and explained all over again.

I am interested in modern philosophy. I don't understand it much better than I do modern art but, at least, I have gathered that it is now the fashion to deny anything save a quite involuntary existence, thus disproving God. Next year, ten years hence, another generation, and perhaps we can disprove that anyone exists at all.

That just takes us back to a very ancient time and a religion—Maya—which had—and still has—gods, and which teaches that all is illusion: our lives and the world in which we live.

True, to some extent; much that we see, much that we think, hear and believe we know, is illusion. But that we do exist is evident. Perhaps this typewriter, the chair upon which I sit, the December season, this house and the tree still waiting to be trimmed, are illusions. If so, they are nice ones and, I would say, harmless. But of my own existence, through and under God I am convinced, however illusory the life I lead. And here the dissenters, having disproved God, will say I am at least a decade behind the times in my thinking—or two weeks if they have thought of something new since the first of December. And if they have ever heard of Elsie Dinsmore, which I doubt (I never much liked her myself), they may call me by her name.

Those who disprove God believe they live without Him. If I tell them *that's* an illusion, they will not believe me.

For me He is not illusion, He is the dispeller of illusion, the Giver of all life, the Reason for it.

Wherever we are, whatever troubles us, the events that disturb and pass, there is always Love. Few of us are, or have been, without it—family, friends—whether or not they are still with us—the dog beside the chair, the cat walking solitary in the moonlight. Few of us are without hope, illusion or not. Few, spurred by necessity too big to be denied, are without courage, and it is, usually, not for ourselves, but for others.

Look at the woman who has been told that presently

she must die, that for her there is no remedy in medicine or surgery. She says, "Do not tell anyone. I am still young. I am able to work. I must see that my children have as much of a future as I can still provide for them."

Is this not courage?

How many people the world over order their affairs from wheel chairs, disciplining their emotions, forbidding pity? Thousands—asking no favor. How many who have never seen, or who have had sight but briefly, exhibit a clearer view of valiance than the sighted? How many, lying in hospitals or in their beds at home, knowing that tomorrow may mean the ultimate silence, speak, to say, "I'm so much better tonight."

Man is a curious mixture of cowardice and bravery, cunning and honesty, selfishness and self-sacrifice. But, when we consider the hundreds we have met, is there not cause for rejoicing? I think so.

Most of us can count upon our fingers those who have failed to stand tall in emergency, their own or another's; or have refused to extend themselves beyond their apparent capacities when it was demanded of them.

Let current philosophers dissent. They cannot disprove to me what I have witnessed.

I do not know the answers to adultery, murder, theft, crime, any delinquency. If I did, I would not be writing a book, late at night in a quiet house; I would be sitting in high places of government, charged with great responsibility. But one thing I do know: that neither God, nor Love, which is part of God, is illusion.

It is growing colder. My windows are fast against it, but it seeps in a little. We have had warmth this December and foolish roses, until well into the month, in sunny sheltered places; but tonight the temperature drops, the furnace goes on more often than usual, and the wind is rising. No matter how modern the new window fittings, the original frames are old; they do not perfectly conform. Maybe that's what's the matter with me: the frame is worn and has lasted too many years to conform to the fashions, however practical they may be.

I am content. I have no wish to withdraw into a past era which, doubtless, nostalgia has colored; I was probably just as annoyed with the times forty years ago as I am, now and then, with these. I have no wish to be preserved in glass or by other means so that I may be projected into the future science tells us is not unforeseeable. If I am to see it, I would prefer a view from another vantage point, where I would have a more comprehensive outlook. If I labor under illusion, it has served me well, and I would not, for anything, relinquish it. If I am Elsie Dinsmore or Polly-anna, that's all right with me.

On the stone terrace, the tree stands in a large bucket of water and will, in a day or so, be set up; the boxes of ornaments are now in the library. I fall over them every time I go past into the living room. Within a few days I shall have a quiet evening, trim the tree, listen to the carols and, if Scrooge bounces out of my radio, I shall firmly turn him off. . . . A person is, after all, entitled to a few preferences.

The packages have started to arrive, and all of mine that

had to be mailed have been sent. This year, I managed to do things on time. On Christmas Eve, my son, Stephen, Peggy, his wife, and their small Steve (who is nevertheless too big for me to lift) will come from a little distance; my daughter, Hervey, and her children, Faith and Laura, from a shorter. The children will be festively fed, small Steve put to bed and the little girls to nap. Then Gussie, who presides over the kitchen on occasion, will give the grown-ups—if we are grown up—supper, and we will admire the tree and exchange gifts.

On Christmas Day, Stephen and company will have left. Hervey will have gone home, too, but she will return with the children later. I shall have a quiet day alone from morning until early evening. I shall take my coffee into the living room, sit by the big window at the pink marble-topped table and immodestly admire my decorations. And have time to think about Christmases past, in Scrooge parlance.

I do not remember the three in New Rochelle where I was born. The first I recall was in an apartment in New York City; and then, a succession in various houses and apartments in Brooklyn where my parents and I, and later my sister, lived. There were two Christmases in the country at my father's farm; and another, shortly after my wedding, in Puerto Rico. (I could not believe it was Christmas because of palm trees.) And after that, Christmas in the Bay Ridge section of Brooklyn, with a child of my own. Then another child, too young to know about Christmas. And many holidays in still another part of Bay Ridge, where ships sailed the Narrows, and there were four children to discover Christmas. I shall think of those in the New Canaan house, and of my friend, Henry, who always gave us our trees, coming Christmas morning to see if we had done justice and bringing always a great armful of giant pansies, which he raised. And of another Henry, who made our gardens for us; of the wreaths he created, the Christmas cactus he grew. I have never had one since; I think with delight of their lovely red fluted bells.

I shall think of Christmas at Johns Hopkins and the tree we trimmed there for Ann; and of one after we moved to this house; it was not spent here but with friends, in Saranac Lake, all snow and stars. Since we moved, this is the seventh Christmas.

Toward evening Hervey will return with the little girls, who will have had their dinners; and the friends of whom I have often spoken, Raymond Burns, the clergyman who tells me things I frequently put into books, and his wife, Henrietta, will come for dinner. The children will speak their greetings and go off to nap, and we will say our Christmas grace at table.

It's too far off. It's much too soon. It will pass like a comet across the heavens and be gone.

But *that's* illusion. It will never be gone, this Christmas or any other, because each is in my heart and my memory, and each has, a little, shaped me for the next.

God rest you merry . . . !

TWO

January

WINTER IS AS PRODIGAL OF BLOWING WHITE AS MAY WHEN the fruit tree is in blossom. Winter blooms white in snow and cloud. May dawns shine with dew; but January mornings are bright with frost and, often, perilously brilliant with ice. May is so lavish with singing birds that, after a while, we forget to listen. But winter's birds have a little song, a sudden whistle, and these bring sharp awareness and wonder; for in spring birds are a dime a dozen; in winter, worth a king's ransom.

So now I can stand and look at a great bush by my doorway, bare of leaves but always trimmed with birds, for it affords shelter and, for a long time, berries. The blue jay who, in spring, afflicts me with his greed at the feeders, his hostile attitude toward fellow birds, and whose screeching offends the ear, becomes, in winter, a personage of startling beauty, his vigorous shriek cleaving with sound the heavy gray of the winter atmosphere. In spring, the nesting cardinals retreat to the woods and the male sings to his wife from a high, unseen branch; but in winter they come to the doorstep: the gentleman wearing red, with a black bow tie; the lady, a soft dull yellow, brushed with red, and having a bright scarlet beak as if she had taken to extra lipstick.

The common sparrow with his busy chirp is much like some of us; there are so many sparrows, each with special characteristics—in summer we listen for those who sing most beautifully but rarely bother to distinguish one from another. The junco, who goes somewhere else in summer, returns with the first cold, in flocks, hooded in black and clothed in gray. The nuthatches are bluer than we remember, and if one is walking upside down on a nearby tree trunk, it brightens the dreary hour. As for the chickadees, they are as pretty and cheerful as good children; they are also fearless and their speech admonitory. Now and then they confuse the listener by speaking exactly like a phoebe. Come spring, they'll have modest song, but in winter they talk big; almost bigger than themselves.

All during the winter I watch for the pheasant and note the flight of ducks or the blackness of a crow against the falling snow; and when, now and then, a sudden bird appears who really ought to be somewhere else—the towhee, the raspberry-colored finch—I worry about him. I never worry about any in spring.

What I am trying to say is that every season has its special beauty and compensations. It may be too icy to go out upon the treacherous roads, we may have to break an engagement we wanted to keep, but there are warmth and safety indoors, windows to look through, perhaps a fire on the hearth, books, and—unless the ice has torn down the overhead wires —a telephone.

As in late autumn, with the first snow, we gratefully think each day we are one day nearer spring, so with the blazing of the sun and the running feet of grass we can, I think, be grateful for the inevitable coming of winter.

God's plan is never one of monotony. He works through contrasts: the seasons, tropic and arctic regions, seas and rivers, deserts and wastelands. He works to bring about good; to teach compassion. Some have said that God is impersonal, indifferent to suffering. There have been times when I, too, have thought so. There are moments in the life of every man when, unable to explain the Plan satisfactorily to himself, he wonders why is there loss, tragedy, destruction of peoples, the sorrow of the innocent?

If we knew why, we would have achieved our identification with the Plan itself.

Out of fire and flood comes the strength to rebuild, the impulse to share unselfishly, to comfort and sustain, the great drive to compassion felt by one or many people. Out of loss comes the growing into knowledge that—past the material— there is no real loss. Out of surrender, I believe, a conquering is attained; out of the violence of emotions, the noise of self-pity and distraction, we learn quietude.

In the schools we attend as children and young adults there are classes, teachers, books, instruction and interpretation, but the best, most sympathetic teacher cannot study for us or pass our examinations. If we fail, we are permitted to try again, but that can't go on indefinitely because we can't stay in the same grade forever and someone has to graduate. The apple for the teacher, in whatever form, is usually accepted but not as bribery. In the larger school of spiritual advancement some things are much the same: we have instruction, starting with the parents who speak to us of God, and of right and wrong; we have our own inner spiritual guidance, some with more awareness than others. Some call it direct God-guidance, some the conscience and others merely ethical behavior. Whatever it is, each has it in varying degrees. But our lessons are not learned for us, nor are the solutions given us on a silver platter; we still have to pass our own examinations.

In this school, which begins when we are born and which, I am certain, doesn't end when we die, there are, I suspect, grades, if no ultimate graduation. There is never a possibility of cheating because our neighbor's questions may not be asked of us, so what use would his answers be? Also there are no holidays, and classes are never dismissed. I suppose the great compensation is that, no matter how often we fail, we are never struck from the rolls and there is no such thing as being expelled.

God moves, we are told, in a mysterious way, but how mysterious also is man, trying and failing, advancing, falling back, and again moving on; never wholly known to, or understood by, himself or even the person closest to him on earth. But known completely, understood completely, by God alone, Who patiently moves through His creations.

[35]

One of the lessons we learn at an early age and which we keep on learning is prayer. Books are written on how to pray, but I believe that each must find his own method. Most of us start with the simple, familiar prayers, and progress to our own. Some use formalized prayer all their lives; others speak their hearts, however childishly, as they speak to an earthly father, if they love and have confidence in him. It is not hard to learn to be grateful for what we receive and to offer thanks for it. It is very hard to be grateful and offer thanks for what we have not received, for what has been withheld.

When, as a child, you want something and your parents say "No," if they are wise, they explain why. Usually you resent it, explanation or not, unless you are a great deal more reasonable than most children. As an adult you can usually look back and realize how good for you was the withholding. You have perhaps by then withheld something from a child of your own.

Therefore, as we continue our spiritual schooling, we do eventually learn to be grateful for what was not given, the prayer which we say was not answered.

Oh, but it was answered, even though it may take us years to learn how. And by then perhaps we have learned to ask only, "Give, Lord, what is best for me."

That's a prayer which has been ascribed to Socrates, although I think it was said by an anonymous poet. I have quoted it before. But be patient with me, for it bears repeating.

In essence it asks that we be given good, whether or not

we pray for it, and denied the evil for which, unwittingly, we may have prayed.

Now that it is again January, I find I have no great desire to look ahead, or to make special resolutions. The ones I make every day (and usually break) suffice. I find that my interest lies in looking back and attempting to see what I have gained or lost, learned or failed to learn. This is not done by sitting in a comfortable chair or lying in a pleasant, warm bed and casting out for memories, as with a seine. One nets very little that way. It is done through many hours, when you reconstruct a past year, bit by bit, as if you assembled a jigsaw puzzle, once solved, then taken apart and now to be put together again.

Curious how much of the jigsaw you have forgotten.

Tonight, in a house silent except for the sound of the typewriter—for the wind has died down after a January thaw which threatens more snow—I am minded to stop typing and take from a bookshelf a little hourglass. It doesn't really measure an hour. It's an egg timer or telephone-call warden, and it measures just three minutes.

I have turned it; the three minutes are run, grains of sand through a narrow aperture, and they will never come again, or, not exactly the same three minutes.

We are all acquainted with siderial time—something I have never understood when I crossed the date line, lost a day, and found a different new day on the way back. We all understand psychological time—the drag of anticipatory moments, the rushing past of happy hours—but how much do we understand of timelessness?

The three minutes I have just measured out are apparently gone, yet somewhere they are registered: they are etched into my subconscious, grooved indelibly on a record. Could I, now, play that record back, I would find that, although I thought I did nothing, watching the sand grains run, I did a great deal. For three minutes I was thinking, and whatever I or anyone else may think, at any time at all, however idle-seeming, is important.

In three minutes anyone can experience a great happiness or tragedy; in three minutes a man can lose his life; a signature can be set to a piece of paper which will bring war to the world or gladden it with peace; in three minutes any of us can wreck a reputation, or meet a stranger who will alter our lives or whose life will be altered by us. In three minutes we can refuse, or give, compassion; fall in love, fall out of it. In three minutes many things can happen.

A year is composed of many times three minutes and all of them bring responsibility. Looking ahead, while hopeful, can also be somewhat futile. Let us therefore look back. I do not know you, so I cannot look back with you, only for myself.

Looking back, I wonder how much I have accomplished in a year's time. Usually I am in the red when I set up my accounts—perhaps more than I think; perhaps less. For the true books are kept elsewhere.

I'm always in the red in terms of spiritual accomplishment as, in common with many people, I do not always follow the guidance of the higher self, the spirit within me, or the spiritual forces beyond. I generally know what I should, or should not, do, but I certainly manufacture excuses for failure. The simplest rule for true guidance is also the most profound. It begins "Do unto others . . ." Try that every day and see how often you fail!

In terms of emotional achievement I believe I am slightly in the black, for the past year has brought fear and anxiety for those I value more than myself. This has led me inward to the in-dwelling Christ and upward to the Father. And bestowed upon me answered prayer. Passionately to fear is in itself no accomplishment; it isn't something you choose voluntarily; but what you *do* with your fear can be constructive, and I hope that I was.

As far as creative accomplishment is concerned, I am a fraction in the black, having returned to work I thought I could never do again. I felt my way into, and through it, and whatever the results, to have been able to write at all was something of a major feat.

Actually, looking back from a year's beginning is an attempt to see the panorama of what has gone before. But looking back at each day's end, over hours, rather than months, gives a more valid close-up, and if we would do that today, tomorrow would be better. But we don't. We are too tired or sleepy or annoyed by something which has, or has not, taken place. The conscious mind is full of small daily pleasures and disappointments, the worries of the moment, the glancing or crushing blow.

"Do unto others as you would be done by" sounds easy but is hard. It has the widest possible range—from not criticizing people or gossiping about them to the sacrificial acts. I sometimes think people make a narrow, self-seeking interpretation of the Golden Rule. For instance, we like to receive gifts, so we give. That is doing unto others, literally and materially, what we would like them to do for us, isn't it?

I have lately thought that the interpretation could well be: Do unto others as you would have them do unto you—*according to God's will*.

Last summer, because I went travelling with friends I had only six weeks on Cape Cod. Those weeks were as unlike the two summers before as possible. Three summers ago I went to the Cape for three months, to try to find my balance, to luxuriate in the understanding of those near me, and endeavor to work. We had a season of hot weather, hurricanes, and I learned, a little, to relax, wind or no. That was the summer I tried to return to fiction writing; I worked hard and didn't do well but, at least, I tried. The summer before last there were disturbances ranging from the serious illness of my older son to the things which always go wrong in your own house when you're away from it. And the weather was different, a cold rainy June, a few days of heat, and then sunny, cool and windy days.

No summer ever repeats itself. It is said that history does, but not the day-by-day history of the average man or woman. There is always something different.

Last summer brought six weeks of rest, and water too cold for me to have any desire to swim. One compensation in reaching maturity plus, is that you don't mind being called chickenhearted. In my youth I braved freezing water and, after the numbness passed, rather liked it. Not any more.

My younger friend, Gladys Taber, strides out with a swift, almost frightening determination, no matter how cold it is. She and her Irish setter have mermaid blood. But I am content, while my toes turn blue, to paddle around in the shallows and pick up driftwood or look for shells.

One summer I arrived at the little house on the Cape too late to prune the roses which grow in such profusion down the bank, past the sand terrace. I was sorry to miss them. I like to cut them for the house, in bud and blossom, which is a species of pruning, and later to prune with severity. I remember the summer I did just that, hacking away at as many wild straggling branches and perished flowers as I could reach without falling down the bank myself. The growth was undisciplined in all directions and choked by honeysuckle and bindweed, which is also called morningglory. Both are pretty, but they kill the roses.

As I worked, I began to think of all the untamed growth within ourselves: luxuriant, also choked, and, certainly, in all directions. As I reached out, tugged, and was scratched, I thought of personal attributes, attractive to the outward view but harmful to rewarding growth. There is, for instance, the desire to please everyone, which can run riot and stifle the growth of character. Like the roses burgeoning wildly, character without true direction is not reliable. And the honeysuckle quality of eager amiability can cause trouble. Cutting back, and out, is the answer.

Perhaps January is not the time to prune roses, but it is as good a time as any in which to take a long, hard look at oneself and do some emotional and mental pruning.

This is not as easy as whipping about among the roses with gloves and shears. The latter is comparatively simple even if you come out panting, sunburned and scratched, as I did. Lopping off undisciplined branches, uprooting any alien growth which kills, takes time and may never be entirely accomplished. But to look is good; to take the shears of determination and realism is better; to bring some order out of chaos is best of all.

January is an odd month. Christmas with its lovely excitement and much lovelier inner meaning has gone. The tree is down (although I leave my outdoor wreaths up all winter, to shine green and brave against whatever weather and to attract the birds). You do not yet look to spring— but think ahead only to February holidays like Valentine's Day, if you are sentimental as I am.

Most people compare a new year to a blank sheet of paper upon which one may write for good or evil. I don't. Every day in the year is that, in a sense, for every day of our lives, even if we live to be a hundred, we have a choice. No page of a new year is entirely blank, because what has happened during the year before must be carried over, as one carries over figures in a ledger. No one moves, as it were, into a new, unspotted mental and spiritual house. Just as a person does not entirely change his personal atmosphere when he moves physically a thousand miles, so none among us can move into January First as innocent as a baby. For, in the ledger of the new year so much is carried over, not only from last year but from those preceding: items which are negative, items which are positive; notations of qualities—kindness and cruelty, generosity and meanness, fault-finding and understanding. There are too many to list, but each of us knows, or should, what we take with us into the new year.

And there is no use wishing any season could be exactly like the one before. No pattern is duplicated. There is no use wishing we could start over, because we cannot. We have to go on from where we are.

Half the battle lies in overcoming what has gone before, but which remains in our consciousness through indifference or habit or both. I suppose the real purpose of a new year is to get us to go ahead, no matter what we have to take with us. For if any new day or year holds anything, it is promise and hope. There are burdens which will eventually slip from us, not always through our own efforts, but simply because the time has come to put them down, perhaps because new ones must be assumed. There are always things which can be rectified.

One of the wisest and most understanding men I ever knew once said that the Land of Might-Have-Been is the greatest of all illusions. To sit by a window or walk on a road thinking of how different things would now be if we had only done or had not done thus and so, makes no sense. For we didn't, and we can't go back and live it over again. It takes a long time to realize that Might-Have-Been is a fairy tale, and even longer to know that we can't live other people's lives for them.

I think we will all have a good year if we forget what might have been last year or a decade or quarter century ago. I think we might have a wonderful year if we do some personal pruning in our lives. And I am absolutely certain that we will have the brightest year we have ever known if, during it, we do unto others as we would have them do to us and always, always do God's most loving will.

What I have learned from the year past is something about miracles—miracles of healing and answered prayer and unexpected happy things. Each came quietly and simply, on tiptoe, so that I hardly knew it had occurred.

All this makes me realize that miracles are everyday things. Not only the sudden, great good fortune, wafting in on a new wind from the sky. They are almost routine, yet miracles just the same.

Every time something hard becomes easier; every time you adjust to a situation which, last week, you didn't know existed; every time a kindness falls as softly as the dew; or someone you love who was ill grows better; every time a blessing comes, not with trumpet and fanfare, but silently as night, you have witnessed a miracle.

I see now how things even up, how they are squared away, and how they balance under the law of love and justice. No year of life is emotionally, spiritually or even materially, all drought or all rainfall; nor is it all sun. The road turns a little every day, and one day there's a sudden twist we didn't dream was there, and for every loss there is somewhere a gain, for every grief a happiness, for every deprivation a giving.

Some people think of God as far away. I believe that He is close to us every day. The Master's path is long, straight and difficult because, although to love, to give and to serve sounds easy, actually it's very hard, and if we have achieved even the shortest step upon the path, then He, indeed, travels with us.

Always we have to face failures, shortcomings, and the times when it seems impossible to move forward. But if the effort is there, if, no matter how often we fail, we try again, then something of value is accomplished.

Confucius said—though I can't quote exactly—that, when we *think* we are being generous or kind, we are not.

There is a truth to mull over. The natural gesture of wholly spontaneous kindness is the only one that counts. The kindest people I have known were those who, if told they were being kind, would be astonished and burst into laughter. They are kind because they operate not from the mind but from the spirit, as spontaneously as a flower blooms, or the rain falls or the sun shines. They can't help it. They don't stop to think about it. It is part of their personalities. They have to give, be and do because that's the way they are.

I have known great "kindnesses" lavishly bestowed, even with self-sacrifice, but with a thought back of them which approximates, "What's in it for me?" In that case the answer is: Absolutely nothing!

As the years pass and my topknot grows whiter, I am certain that the things I can recall having done for people are of no moment. I hope that, somewhere along the line, there were up-welling acts and words which *I* have forgotten but which someone may remember . . . not in gratitude at this distance . . . perhaps not even remembering me or my name, but remembering just because, at the time, kindness was a little miracle. I have had such things happen to me, and I remember.

I remember the words of the first editor who ever encouraged me. I remember letters from strangers along the years. I remember the first literary agent who taught me how to work. I remember a child running to put his arms around my knees in a gesture of pure love. I remember isolated words, spoken without planning or thinking, which changed the face of the world for me. I remember, though the persons who did these things have forgotten.

When you count on your personal ledgers the gains and losses of the past year, do not forget to count the little miracles—if any miracle is ever little.

It has been suggested that the new year should begin on Labor Day, because three holidays in a row can be wearing: Thanksgiving first, and the turkey hardly consumed when it's Christmas; and then before the tree comes down or the thank yous are written, suddenly it's New Year's and anything wonderful can happen.

We are so accustomed to the old New Year, I don't suppose anyone would want to start a new year early in September, but arbitrary dates don't really matter much. Thanksgiving should be every day and Christmas every day and Easter every day; the purpose back of each, not the traditional celebration. And surely a new year should begin each morning when we open our eyes to a new day, a whole twenty-four hours during which we live a miniature year. In any day anything can happen, and in almost every hour we make small decisions and big, and have, with each, a choice of good or evil. Thus a day is shaped and after that, it's tomorrow and another day, another twenty-four-hour "year."

Regarding the year just past and those before it, I am conscious of having strayed and erred, of sins of omission as well as commission. But I am not one who would wish to live life over again. For I doubt that I would do so differently. Only by trial and error is any lesson learned. One of the hardest to learn is to be grateful for the hardest ones.

I think that on every day of the new year we should pray for the leaders of all governments. For those who are good need strength and sustaining, and those who may be evil need spiritual enlightenment. Only by such light can leaders and their people see the path ahead.

This is a lesson soberly to be learned. Jesus told us to pray for our enemies, for those who did not love us. It is not hard to pray for an impersonal enemy, one we never see or know; to pray for all leaders, however hostile-seeming to our country's interest, is no difficult task, unless that enemy is made personal to us through the suffering of someone we love at the hands of men representing that leadership. Ah, then it's hard, I know. And so one comes to the realization that it is the personal enemy for whom we find it almost impossible to pray.

"I can't pray for her," someone said to me recently. "I know I should. I know I should surround her with thoughts of love, but I'm so *mad* at her!"

I suspect she has to pray for herself, then, and forgive

[47]

herself for being mad, before she can pray for her personal enemy.

So, it's a new year, and I have been looking back, not ahead, yet in a way, it *is* looking ahead . . . hoping to do a little better, to see a little more clearly.

Praying, we usually ask too much. I know I do. Sometimes we even demand. I think I am learning to ask enough for the moment—not for the whole year, utterly veiled in mystery; not even for the week, the month ahead; but just for today.

Jesus said it all when He told us to pray: "Give us this day our daily bread."

That bread is not only material, it is spiritual; in asking for it, we ask for a sufficiency of strength, courage, hope and light. Enough courage for the step ahead—not for the further miles. Enough strength for the immediate task or ordeal. Enough material gain to enable us to meet our daily obligations. Enough light to see the path—right before our feet.

With sufficiency from day to day, the new year will be happy.

THREE

February

FEBRUARY IS A MONTH BOTH FOR REMEMBERING AND FOR thinking ahead. During February, in New England the worst can happen weatherwise and often does; but then the hearts of the skiers—who are, to me, inexplicable people—are gladdened. In February, shop windows exhibit miniature log cabins and also little hatchets (for the cherry tree that, we are now told, never existed). I have for Abraham Lincoln a most profound admiration and for George Washington great esteem. Perhaps I understand one better than the other; in any case, I admire both. But I am sure that, being men of understanding, they would not be offended when I say that February, for me, means Valentine's Day.

Valentine's Day, when I was a child, meant lace-frilled paper sentiment, and sometimes, I grieve to recall, the allegedly comic valentine which, the reverse of funny, sent many a child, young or old, weeping to whatever sanctuary she was sure of finding. . . . If she were fortunate, it would be a sympathetic mother.

Nowadays, the comic valentine is coming back. If you wait long enough, everything returns, including the most unbecoming and hideous of female fashions. Today's enveloped stabs are less crude than yesterday's, but even more wounding.

However, they are in the minority among the valentines which await pen, ink and stamp at the greeting-card counters. They are now designed for everyone—not only wife, husband, sweetheart, brother and sister and children, but for cousins, aunts and uncles, even one's most distant inlaws.

I like to buy and send them. I always have, but in recent years Valentine's Day came to have deep meaning for me. I shall always be grateful for it.

Not far from the house there is a growing valentine. For one October we planted three Christmas roses—I don't know the Latin name. I suppose they aren't roses at all, but that's what they are called. Sturdy and astonishing, the advertisement assured, they bloom from December through February, come snow, sleet or hail, "when established."

Since then, their valiant leaves, and their petals, whiter than the snow, have been discernible, in their short season, under the rooted feet of evergreens, and I know that my doubtful moments during the planting were unjustified. Then, I was certain that the directions were wrong. If those strange little roots, attached to woebegone stems, were really to flower, wouldn't they, especially in winter, need as much sun as possible? But, no, the directions read firmly: "Plant in shade, preferably under trees or among ferns."

That made little sense. What trees cast shade in December, and where are the ferns? Then I thought of the pines, so under them the "roses" went. But the next December I went out to look for holly berries and never thought of roses, Christmas though they were called; in January, it seemed a long way to the stand of pine. In February, given one of the bright days the woodchuck fears, I put on boots and went out and found the "roses," as a valentine.

Let me send you a valentine from the heart, as all real ones should be sent. (I remember a five-cent one, sent on a snowy day to a mailbox in Florida, which returned to me the most heart anyone has ever given me.)

My valentine for you has to do, not with hearts and flowers, but with directions and compensations.

Consider the Christmas roses; however strange the directions appeared, by following them, we had results; but remember, to achieve results, the roots had to be established.

We all must follow directions, and often they seem so wrong we cannot see how we will find our way to growing. Yet to become established through following directions is to be rooted in certainty.

There are many outward directions which, as children, we are taught to respect; these deal with ethics, morals and conventions. There are also inward directions which have to do with spirit, and if all are followed, establishment is accomplished.

I think of an integrated person as an established one, with roots deep in the good earth, and growth, as in a tree, aspiring to heaven. Anyone too lightly rooted in earth, a little unsteady, a trifle unbalanced, can easily fall before a storm. Not to many of us is true mysticism accorded, and to live wholly in the clouds is not conducive to balance. The integrated person understands that, having been endowed with life in this world, however difficult or exasperating, he must establish himself in it . . . and look toward the far sky in aspiration and gratitude.

As the Christmas rose, battling upward through the snow in a small miracle of bloom, is compensation, on a dismal day, for the winter not ended, so—as we move through our lives, seeing always through a glass darkly—compensations flower all about us, whatever the temperature of the particular moment is registering in our hearts.

But if we do not look for the compensations, we do not find them.

Some months ago a young man, dying, said of his mother: "She was so wonderful—she was always looking view-ward."

The clergyman who listened, afterward told me.

I said, "What a wonderful sermon that would make!"

He replied, "So few, comparatively speaking, hear a man's sermon. More people will read the written word. *You* think about it."

So I have thought, and now I write, in tribute to a young man, to his mother, who was always looking view-ward, and to the friend who told me about it.

In my study there are five windows. Three give south over yard, knoll and millstone birdbath, to stone walls, trees and beyond. The two which face the west look past the iron work surrounding stone steps we never use, to a so-called lawn, so heavily caparisoned with great maples that little grass grows there. Walk across it and there's another wall, in front of which are lilac and forsythia bushes and pines. Down along the stone wall is the usual strip of grass and the winding public road. Directly across, there used to be an old barn.

From these west windows there is no spectacular view except of the sunset, which is superb, particularly in winter, or a sky full of stars, or frosted by the moon. There are, of course, trees, which, for me, are enough, for trees are wonderful to behold whatever the season. The barn, when we moved here, seemed something of an obstruction, but I rather liked it. It wasn't very attractive or old enough to be interesting; nor was it used for the original purpose, but for storing things belonging to the owners.

I was told that the owners contemplated destroying the barn, and people who came to see me would say with some disdain, "That old thing. Wouldn't you think they'd tear it down?" But I grew quite fond of the structure standing almost at road's edge, sturdy, having weathered storms, hurricanes, blizzards and the depredations of animals. Also it was a sort of guidepost when I had to give directions to people coming to see me for the first time. I have difficulty distinguishing right from left (unless I look for my wedding ring) and therefore am apt to entangle everyone in wrong roads. I once gave two sets of directions simultaneously, one to a Long Island friend, one to my agent; my Long Islander arrived with ease, and on the following day my agent turned up. She, too, had followed directions, but I had reversed hers; when she took a left, it should have been a right and vice versa. But with that old barn opposite—if I could get people that far—they couldn't miss.

Now the barn is gone. One day, perhaps two years ago, a friend came in and announced, "They have started to tear down the barn." And so they had. By evening it was as roofless as the sky. Since then the bulldozers and well drillers have been in, together with carpenters, plasterers and masons, so there are three houses, not where the barn was but in back of the site and to the side. A little road has crept in, and children come running out and wait for the school bus in the morning. So there is less view than ever.

The vantage point is everything, and there's a compensation. What you look from makes a difference in what you see. Look from a mountain, from a plain, from a beach, from a window—what you see is conditioned by the point from which you look.

The house on Cape Cod is a view-ward-looking house. From the desk there, under a huge window, I can glance up to see fields, pines, bayberry bushes, the inlet's waters, the houses on the Heights beyond, and the ocean. The other big windows are on either side of a couch. You can't see from those if you are sitting on the couch . . . and not much, if sitting elsewhere, but, rising, you can look across the sand terrace, down the tumble-rose hill to the curving beach and the Mill Pond; and the view of the Heights alters.

In my own house, in any season, if the day is clear, I can see from the sun porch or the south windows of my bedroom what seems a far horizon. It is the dark floating outline of a small portion of Long Island, and between me and that outline, there is a bright glimpse of water. In winter there is more Island and more Sound, for the screening trees are bare.

It is inevitable that men look view-ward, from the sea to the land, from the land to the sea. People coming from the city into the country exclaim more over views than anything else. One of the few good short stories I ever wrote concerned a view which I saw as I drove along a high country road. The man who lives in the city, if he is fortunate enough to live high above the streets, and perhaps to have a terrace, will immediately show you his view, mainly beautiful by night.

About now someone is going to ask: "What of the people who live in the steaming or shivering darkness of tenement and slum? Where is their view?"

Their outward view is just that—outward.

Going by train into the city one passes through unsavory sections. There the buildings climb a few stories, and instead of a terrace there is a fire escape. Children sit on the fire escapes in warm weather, looking out; men and women lean from the windows to watch the passer-by below, or to contemplate a brave red geranium in its pot upon a sill.

All over this country there are houses huddled close together—not only in the city—where the view may be of the neighbors' activities, a scrap of grass, a few bushes or a tree. But somehow there is always a view of some sort.

Many people dislike autumn, thinking of it as the approaching death of flowering things. Yet from autumn's sudden blaze of glory, the view-ward look is toward the spring.

Many people dislike winter, and not all can escape it, as they may wish to, by fleeing to warmer climates. But winter also has its enchantment. One can look to the star snow falling, each of the innumerable flakes differently fashioned. Or watch blue shadows on the snowbank, silver moonlight upon the white brilliance of ice. One can look to the bare branches of the trees patterned in unconcealed beauty against the sky. And one can look also underfoot. For beneath the frozen ground the spring is waiting.

When spring comes, the apple blossoms invite wonder; but people soon mourn to see them fade and fall, the lilacs slip from purple and white into brown. But after the apple blossom, there is the fruit; after the flowers' departure, the new green shoots.

Looking view-ward with the physical eye is wonderful: to see the seasons swing, to watch from many windows the differing outlooks, is to perceive, however myopically, the incomparable Plan. But to be able to look view-ward with the mind, the heart and the spirit is something for which we should pray.

The young man who spoke of his mother was not speaking of her physical sight.

Looking view-ward means taking the long view. It requires great self-discipline to look view-ward from sorrow and loss, or from the common anxieties and tumults of every-day life.

I know a woman who learned to look view-ward when, to her great grief, a handicapped child was born into her family. Looking from the further distance, she could see what the child had brought into that family: compassion.

It is difficult to look at newspaper headlines with any-thing save the physical eyes. It is hard to look with the inner eye at what seems injustice, unnecessary tragedy, anguish, misfortune—whether our own or that of others.

In many of us the eyes of the spirit are very nearly blind, but to discern the Plan, even dimly, is a step forward into the knowledge of God. Sometimes this knowledge is revealed to us briefly at strange times, in moments of great emotion, in prayer, or just walking along a quiet road and hearing a bird sing. For that split second—and it has hap-pened, I think, at least once in a lifetime to every adult—we feel we are on the verge of complete wisdom, in the heart of the universe. The moment passes and we cannot recapture it, but we are never again quite the same. We have, for a moment, without the physical eyes, looked really view-ward.

No one I know has kicked more against the pricks than I; none has been sorrier for himself than I at times; none has cried out more bitterly and with more resentment at what he thought was injustice; none has felt more inadequate or defeated. Learning to look away, and across and beyond, has been a wonderful experience. I am not very adept at this—perhaps I shall never be—but I have learned to make the effort.

Those who have helped me have my eternal gratitude, which is something they have not asked. And He who has helped me, through these friends, will see that they are repaid.

In everything we are called upon to face, or do, viewward-looking is helpful beyond measure. The big obstacles seem to close all doors and windows; the little ones shut away understanding and compassion or—because we are tired at the day's end and even one task more seems far too much —block off all energy.

I think that to conquer the quite human irritations caused by those of our species who seem to be bore or whiner, dullard or snob, exhibitionist or door mat, the long view inward is the only way—short of incarcerating yourself so you'll never meet anyone who exasperates you. Try wondering if you, too, may not present one of these aspects to other people. Perhaps you present them all, to different people. It is a sobering thought: I have bored just as many people as have bored me. I complain that Mrs. So and So is always talking about her ailments and her troubles, but to how many friends have I confided my own aches, my own upsetments? As for dullards, there are many persons, knowing a great deal more than I, who must think me one. I shudder to contemplate an evening in the company of an expert in electronics—it takes all the technical knowledge I possess to operate a toaster.

And snobbishness is in us all: the ancestor-worshipping

snob, the intellectual snob, the material-possession snob, the talent snob, the name dropper, the hanger-on-the-fringes of whatever seems better than anything else—even the religious snob, who believes that his is the only path to the Creator and thinks himself a long stride ahead of everyone else on that path.

As for being an exhibitionist, who isn't, at one time or another? And the door-mat quality is instinct in even the bravest of us when, dreading quarrel or argument, the loss of friendship, or a spoiled social hour, we keep silent, though something—or someone—in which we profoundly believe is being attacked.

One of the compensations in growing old is that, if we have not been born with the view-ward-looking heart, we sometimes attain it.

Many people say that there are no compensations for aging unless it be grandchildren. Some, perhaps, don't consider them a bonus. But I have found a number of compensations, despite protesting joints and the realization that, in even as healthy a creature as I, there are limits to physical endurance. However, I have long looked into mirrors and steadfastly refused to believe what I see. The clock of the mind stands at eighteen or twenty, at the very most at thirty, and when the mirror cries, "Liar!" it's a shock.

But there is the fact that, as you grow older, you don't *have* to do all people expect of you. You needn't whip around the way you did when you were thirty. People regard your graying hair and think: Perhaps it *was* unkind to ask her to make the eighteenth speech this past month!

More important, of course, is that one's judgments become less quick and cruel. You aren't as apt to pin other people down with the sharp, pointed word. You're willing to live for whatever time is left. You begin slowly to lose the craven, though human, fear and resentment of death. People you love have gone before, and if your own life is to be a comparatively long one, you will one day be tired enough to let go of it, however dear it's been. Surely, as you grow older you grow stronger, if not in body, then in faith.

In my case, I have long since relinquished the desire for great prestige, for enormous success. I know it wasn't to be, so I do the best I can. There are still books I want to write. I don't know that I can, but I do know that I couldn't thirty, twenty, even ten years ago. Now I can at least try. And that, too, is compensation, the daring to try but without the tremendous drive of ambition, feeling you've learned a little along the way and that there's still more to learn.

When people fail you or hurt you, you feel less resentment than when you were young. You try instead to walk in their shoes, to discover what troubles or hurts them. You don't think the world has come to an end simply because you've had a disappointment. The hurt is there, of course, but when you look back on the bitterness you experienced years ago in a like situation, you marvel at your misdirected anguish.

As the catalogue directions promised that the roses we planted would bloom "when established," so, I think, we all bloom when we are established in God. Unless we are firmly rooted with faith in Him, we wither and die, even though outwardly we may live for many years. On my bedside table, as well as on my desk, there is a small Bible. So at any time of day or night—while I am working, or resting in bed, or when I wake, I can put out my hand, turn the pages and find my "directions"—those which will assure me of sun and rain, of nourishment, of growth and bloom, and, always, of everlasting life.

I cannot truthfully say that I always follow the directions to the letter, and I am afraid not even in spirit. I have known people who did, and do, as nearly as is humanly possible. I have also known those who *thought* they did, and that kind of thinking engenders a holier-than-thou attitude which can be most exasperating.

Certainly the view-ward look should be inward as well as outward?

Last June I flew to London for a week to see my close friends, Storm Jameson, the writer, and her husband, Guy Chapman, educator and historian. I love them very much and it was wonderful to be again in London, my favorite city of all I have ever seen, and in weather which was really June. In a week's time I saw and did a great deal, even driving to Oxford, which last time I had missed as the roads were washed out; and, of course, returning to St. Paul's, the cathedral, as dear to me spiritually as the house in which I live is physically.

The last time I was there it was snowing, and a charming Christmas service was being held for children, so we could not wander about or go up to the Whispering Gallery.

This time, on a sunny day, we saw the plans for the Jesus Chapel dedicated to American boys, which is to be back of the high altar, and the book in which their names are inscribed. Storm asked if I wished to see the Whispering Gallery. I knew it was up, but not how far, and said yes. To my astonishment I found that I was climbing 358 winding steps. Every so often there was a landing on which I panted like a fish out of water. Once we reached the Whispering Gallery, we might as well, she said, go to the Stone Gallery. I thought that would be just a few steps more. It was quite a few—117! But, oh, the view of London!

Coming down was worse for me, always unsteady on my feet, and I was envious of 177 chaperoned school children who actually ran down those stairs.

On emerging after private prayer in St. Dunstan's Chapel, we stood on the broad steps and listened to a royal regiment band. At certain seasons, one such band plays there every Thursday from noon until two. People wander up from all over Fleet Street, sit on the steps or stand outside. It is a delightful custom.

Flying home, I had only a brief glimpse of Ireland like a great carpet below me, but I thought of the view from the Stone Gallery and how London lay below, all around it, and how different it is from the restricted view one sees when walking or driving through the multitudinous streets.

It's the same with the inner view, I daresay, and so I

wonder. Can we not try to look view-ward with the inner eye at ourselves, at all whom we encounter, and at circumstances and situations? Look beyond, look beneath, look within—for every time we overcome the restricted view the darkness somewhat recedes; the Plan emerges, however dimly, and we are looking view-ward, toward God.

I seem to have wandered away from directions, establishment, from Christmas roses, and Valentine's Day. Most women digress and I am no exception, in thinking, either silently or aloud; in talking, either publicly or privately. One thought flows into another, and I find myself, apparently, many mental miles from where I began. But not so many after all. For, when you stop to consider it, there is first the direction, then the establishment, then the growing up toward the sun—which is a looking view-ward.

So, after all, this is for you, the unknown reader, a Valentine from my heart, as, in February, the Christmas roses bloom and the bright, migrating birds come to the feeders.

March

SINCE THE EMERGENCE OF CIVILIZATION, MAN HAS REGARDED spring as a miracle . . . in its beginning, blossoming and fulfillment. There is about spring a feeling even a totally blind man senses. Yet all seasons bring their gifts—summer, the fruit; autumn, the harvest and flaming tree; winter, the silent snow.

Those who worshipped old gods looked to the return of the spring sun. Those who walk in the Christian faith regard spring as the miracle upon which it is based, the Resurrection.

I am confident that practically everyone believes in miracles, even those who profess to believe in nothing. For the atheist and agnostic do believe in something, even if it's only their own unbelief. In their human relationships, belief in miracles has to be firmly rooted; they must believe in love. Everyone loves or is loved by someone. Each person, however miserable, has somewhere along the road encountered love. And everyone is surrounded, whether or not he believes it, by the unaltering love of God.

Some people would not be astonished if, in their needs, the ceiling opened and showers of negotiable gold descended.

All who believe in miracles are fortunate. They know that, as nothing is impossible to God, the shower of gold is perfectly possible. But some do not wait for it in a dream of wishful thinking. They set about with intelligence and skill to create the lives they wish for themselves and for their families. Skills, intelligences and goals vary widely, but they perform miracles, whether it be a great discovery which benefits mankind as well as the discoverer, or the better job which puts butter on the daily bread or sends a child through college.

I have been rescued more than once from grim material, as well as emotional, difficulties. Each rescue was a miracle, and my gratitude went to the Source of all bounty and spiritual healing.

Every time you look at someone you love and are aware of love in return, that is a miracle. Every time you give freely of yourself, acting upon the higher impulses of your spirit, you are performing one.

A friend of mine recently wrote that good health is the greatest thing in life. I assumed she meant physical health. And when I disputed it, she answered by saying I was wrong; for all sought it, and those who had it (she meant me) didn't appreciate it.

[65]

Health is a marvelous gift; with it we are better able to function usefully. But he who does not look beyond the body's disability is spiritually shortsighted.

Spiritual health, mental health . . . these are more valuable than the body's freedom from pain.

A clergyman, of whom I have often written, told in church one Sunday of a woman, hopelessly crippled in body but as free in spirit and courage as a child running across a field. She works in a hospital; she uses braces and crutches; she is carried to and from the car which takes her there. I believe that those who come to the hospital sorry for themselves must drop their self-pity, as useless equipment, right there on her desk. She does her own housework, even to scrubbing floors. She cared for her mother until the older woman became bedridden, too heavy to lift.

What that crippled woman has is more vital than physical health; what she gives is beyond price.

Only what you give, do you hold. That is a proven truth. In retrospect I can see how over many years I gave without thought. But I don't regret that, when I had the means, I gave.

I can no longer make material gifts in abundance, but I have learned that there are gifts with greater value: thoughtfulness, consideration, prayer and the listening ear of the heart.

However unhappy, frustrating or unsatisfactory to the recipients, life is an inestimable benevolence. You might say: What about the millions living in squalor, imprisonment, misery? They, too, cling to life, for somewhere, somehow, it has given them something. Somewhere they have found love; somewhere there was hope; somewhere compassion came from a stranger: always the lessons which only living can teach.

There is a Plan, and Love and Justice. Paul reminded us that "now we see through a glass, darkly; but then face to face."

Truth remains truth no matter what you do to or with it; whether you seek, find, ignore or repudiate it. In Christianity and many other religions the Golden Rule is implicit. Some don't believe in it, yet preach it; which is hypocrisy. Some believe and preach but do not practice it; this is lip service. But the Rule remains.

There is no reward for preaching what you do not try to practice. Few of us live twenty-four hours a day by the Golden Rule, however much we believe in, and know, its truth. Yet, perhaps, in five minutes of any given day we may express it fully.

Another—and increasingly fashionable—tenet is rooted in truth. Everywhere we hear that we must be tolerant. How I despise this smug word! Let us say *understanding*. "Do not criticize," a wise man said in my hearing; "try to understand." To understand, even in part, is to express respect for the human spirit, respect for the race and religion of an individual, respect for the other man's searching.

By this means, we are told, peace will eventually come to this hysterical, confused planet. For understanding starts in the family, moves through the community, the state and the nation to other nations and the world.

[67]

But how many express the spirit of understanding rather than the letter? We are proud of being "tolerant" in a theoretical sense. But when such tolerance might embarrass us socially or publicly, or when an opinion is at variance with our own, understanding flies out the window.

Many profess themselves lowly; they say they walk in humility. Here again is a spiritual smugness. The people I've known who walked, as far as I could see, in humility, did not crawl; they were upright! They did not think of themselves as humble. They thought of themselves—if at all—as living, forward-going people whose lives were given them as a stewardship.

The world, we are told, is in a perilous state. I suppose people have been saying that for twelve thousand years. Now science is to blow us off the face of the map. Dire things will befall. I noticed, when I went recently to the city for a day, that the tensions and pressures which are afflictions of our era were so tangible I could feel them. I came home with a headache not wholly caused by noise and carbon monoxide.

I am not advocating that we become ostriches and bury our heads in shifting sands (which actually ostriches do not do). It is wise to be realistic, and stupid not to be. But certainly we can overcome our own misgivings enough to prevent them from reaching other people so that we need not add to their tensions by attitudes and shapes of thought.

God's Plan is universal. He knows all about this speck of cosmic dust we call the earth and the space beyond it. It is still true today as Thoreau said in 1851, "Nothing is so much to be feared as fear."

[68]

Now that it's March, do you remember your New Year's resolutions? How are they wearing? Are they a little thin and ragged at the hems, or have they disintegrated? Perhaps they are as whole and workable as they were on January first. If so, you are a better, more resolute person than I, who will not even make resolutions any more. When I used to—I even went so far as to write them down—I discovered that I couldn't, wouldn't, or in any case, didn't, keep them. Sometimes my directions to myself were so easy to follow that I need not have charted them at all. This reminds me of a beloved member of my family who used to give up mashed potatoes for Lent. Secretly, she hated mashed potatoes, but under her mother's bright blue gaze was compelled to eat everything set before her—except such delicacies as she had forsworn during Lent.

To me, New Year's Day seems an artificial division of the calendar; the calendar's been altered several times anyway. Once, the New Year began in spring. . . . I don't know when; March, perhaps. This seems logical, although my emotional new year begins with Christmas.

When I say it's winter, people who live below the Equator recline upon beaches in the baking heat. When I declare it's summer, they wear furs and go skiing.

Perhaps Lent would be a good time not only to give up something but to make resolves. What if it begins in February!

The only way I can hope to keep a fraction of any resolution is to remake it every day; this I do, and while I am conscious of backsliding, shortcoming and willfulness, there's always tomorrow. The seemingly small errors are like bits of ice on the walk; you're looking somewhere else, and first thing you know, you've slipped.

I doubt that I would steal or murder in the usual sense of the words, yet, do I not often steal time from something important, or rob a friend of hope by a careless word? And do I not murder my deepest convictions by keeping silent, in order to maintain peace? And aren't there many ways to kill people other than by gun or dagger, poison or blunt instrument?

I sometimes think the words "blunt instrument," happily employed by mystery writers, are applicable at some time or other to deeds done by us all: the petty crimes of the half-lie or evasion; the cowardice, when for our own social comfort, we defeat equity by silence; the frequent injustice done others; the impatience and bias shown in attitudes, if not words and acts—these snowball into formidable proportions in any year's span.

I've rarely, if ever, gone to bed and looked back on the hours since I rose and found them satisfactory. I have said many times, privately and publicly, in books and articles, that each day we have a choice between good and evil.

Jesus, the great Master, formulated spiritual laws by which to live. Other teachers who preceded and followed Him embodied similar truths in their laws. The greatest Law is Love, and all else stems from it. Every duty brushed aside, all unkindness, indifference and misjudging would be erased if we remained steadfastly obedient to this.

Life is not a succession of smashing major events, good or bad. In every life, major crises arise; no one escapes the sudden eruption of the volcano, the earthquake during which the world falls away from under us, the lightning that strikes without warning. And few go through life without the red-letter periods of happiness and realized dreams. Still, black- or red-letter days are but a handful out of a lifetime, when one considers all the days. For living is, in the main, a procession of small events which add up to an enormous total.

Tearing one's soul apart is sometimes overdone. The continuously guilt-feeling person is not really living in obedience to a law which should be happily expressed, but is inching along in a consciously creeping posture, which is egotism turned inside out. The breast beating of the so-called inferiority complex is a sense of superiority in reverse. Few of us are as good, or as bad, as we profess to believe. There's no more value in going round in a self-castigating hair shirt than there is in being so sure of your ineffable wisdom and purity that you look down at everyone else from eighteen miles up.

Balance is an achievement devoutly to be hoped for. All in nature is in balance. When the floods come, it doesn't seem so, but usually they have followed drought, and eventually the scales will be level. The middle road is the safest, for the high road can make us dizzy with self-importance and the low leads to dark and echoing caves.

Like a coin, everything has two faces . . . evil and good, pain and pleasure, grief and joy. This is trite, but repetition does not make it false. Even the sky is prodigal with contradictions of sun and cloud, and the world is constantly torn between peace and war. Somewhere there is the balance.

Torn, also, are the people of the world. There must be

those who do not know they have conflicts or, if they do, try to solve them. But the hospitals are full of patients who wouldn't, or couldn't, face their confusions until too late to do anything but seek professional help.

Choice, conflict, uncertainty, the hesitant foot upon one path, then another, are perhaps necessary. Each hesitation, each conflict ending in defeat or victory, each path selected, are a part of learning. . . . Often, we do not know, until months or years have passed, what lesson has been learned, or if the grade was failure, passing, good or excellent. I say this from valid experience, as I have always learned the hard way, if at all. But if we aren't upon earth to learn, there would seem to be no real purpose in this existence.

He who has learned from love may also learn from hate. There's another two-sided coin, bright and dark. That which we are quick to condemn in another is often a reflection of something in ourselves, but we still prefer to speak of Mrs. Smith's procrastination, Miss Z's sharp, wounding tongue or Little Miss Muffet's tendency to evade issues.

A resolve to follow the spiritual law, each day, as closely as possible, is a good thing. You will be conscious of failure and of opportunities to which you were blind but, if honest effort is made, there will be honest achievement, however small.

This is the process known as growth.

Do you think it's easy for the tree to bud, to push forward to the leaf, for the stem, thrusting through earth, to accomplish the flower? I'm sure it isn't. Growth is often slow in nature, and in human beings it is, at best, painful.

And all growth must endure heat and cold, storm and struggle. There is no easy way or royal road to anywhere.

I've tried to convince many students of writing of this; but, as a number of people know a number of words, they think it's simple to set one down after another and come out with something everyone will want to read. They don't like being told it isn't that simple.

One of the hardest things to do is to face oneself. I started to say to understand oneself, but I doubt any of us does that completely. It's difficult enough for most, as we become older, to look in a mirror and try to see what is really there. . . . What (literally) in the world, happened to the boy, the girl, the young man, the young woman?

There in the mirror you can see what has happened physically, and even mentally and spiritually, for that, too, is reflected in some measure.

Yet you can't believe it, can you? Because inside yourself you feel no different, though the physical flesh and bones may be somewhat tired.

If we have the courage to look into the mirror of the spirit, which is the true self, it is never a pleasant experience. It is, indeed, a dark seeing, but, now and then, there is a brief revelation of what it will be like when we are truly face to face with ourselves.

For the spirit, being immortal and eternal, matures and grows if we give it any assistance. It can become warped if we do not. I am sure that, in essence, it remains young, for, as St. Paul also said, it is spirit and not flesh. I often think with sorrow of what the human spirit must endure, strug-

[73]

gling to manifest through frail and stubborn, dense and craven flesh; trying to reach the mind we call conscious and the mind we call subconscious, which are of the physical brain; endeavoring to operate through conflicting emotions and desires, through panic, sorrow, despair and sin.

I once heard a great man say that to know one's own spirit, even a little, is to have gained knowledge; and to be guided by it is to have gained wisdom, for the spirit is of God.

He added that Dr. Albert Schweitzer is an example of the man who has listened to his own spirit and, by it, has been guided.

Now, in March, as the year runs away from winter and toward Easter, the rivers are full and the hardier birds appear. The rain blows and the wind, and sometimes the snow descends, but it is a good month in which to renew oneself, as one renews a wardrobe; discarding that which is no longer useful to us or anyone else, tossing aside all which is tattered and unlovely, mending and refurbishing what we are still able to use.

Perhaps we should go through mental attics, trunks and cupboards daily, making provision for renewal. Here, we have laid away old resentments and envies, ancient grudges and self-pityings. Usually we don't think about them, yet they are still there, in the mothballs of memory. They are of no value to us, and no one else wants them; they wouldn't fit anyone else and each has plenty of his own. In order permanently to discard outworn spiritual garments, we must be certain we've outgrown them, and pray that they no longer would fit us if we tried them on.

Introspection is often unpleasant, and too much of it can be dangerous—for you start going around in circles and end where you began. But stock-taking is reasonable and never out of date.

As has everyone else, I have gone to sleep wishing I need never again awaken upon this earth. But wake I always have so far, and whatever situation or anxiety afflicted me, it was usually still there. But sometimes I saw it clearer for repose, and in light, rather than darkness. Often I waken, wondering why I must get up. . . . But get up I do eventually, after prodding myself, and go about my business.

We are all forced to go about our business, day after day, like it or not; and if, at the same time, we can be about our Father's business, our own difficulties considerably lessen.

His business is Love.

I do not mean sentimentality, or lip service, or the saccharine and maudlin, all of which exasperate me. Actually, the basic principle of what we have long termed the "Polly-anna" attitude is good and right; it is only in misuse and misinterpretation that it becomes artificial and mawkish.

Love is not cake. It is nourishing bread, often with a hard crust into which you can set your mental teeth. Its quality is protein strength and vitamin vitality rather than carbohydrate sweetness. Love is the most powerful weapon in this or any world, more powerful than any man has yet devised, or ever will. It is no pliant reed to break beneath the hand, but a strong support, a furthering sort of assistance over the hard spots in the road.

Love is the ability to say "no," when "yes" is not indicated; and to say "yes" when "no" would be betrayal. Love is not blind or deaf; it is the clear-seeing, the clairvoyance, the clear-hearing, the clairaudience of the heart. It is strength, not weakness; constructive, not destructive; and it is healing . . . for with love, we heal ourselves and others.

Such love is an expression of the Love we draw from God, which is freely given that we in our fallible human way may also manifest it. In any form, it is not to be disdained . . . for the spiritual Law of Love is as a tree, with many branches and numberless leaves. Some leaves are misshapen, or not developed; others drift from the branch; some are attacked by enemies from within and without, and no two are exactly alike. But tree, branch and leaf have the same origin, and are thereby nourished. Man's demonstrations of love are as many as the leaves; always he reaches upward to express Love for his Creator, by whatever name he calls Him; he gives personal love to those close to him; and expresses it universally in service, wherever that may take him.

Any love is part of all Love, however misdirected it may seem to us, however transient it may be, however less than ideal.

Love is the power and the glory, and we are given it to follow, as law; we are entrusted with it, as with a stewardship, and required to offer it to those who cross our paths, however briefly, as well as in all our intimate relationships. For this is the gift we return to Him.

To become a source, we draw from the Source, and as we are granted light, so also must we give it. Such is the Law and, if we try to live by it, even failing, we will find that it will never fail us.

Now, as we go into the early spring, under the physical laws of nature we are aware of the cycle of the seasons.

Robert Browning said, in a poem which has become less fashionable to quote than once it was, that "God's in his heaven— All's right with the world."

Fashionable or not, the truth remains. The world, from our limited viewpoint, may not seem right in many ways. Certainly any of us could point out how it could be improved but, if we believe that, whatever has happened or may take place, God is in His heaven, then all *is* right with our personal worlds forever.

What this belief brings is quietude. I often speak of it and am, as often, asked exactly what I mean.

It is hard to express. I think of beautiful words such as "tranquillity," "serenity" and "peace of mind," as names of outward qualities; physical in the sense that they are desirable expressions of body and brain. "Quietude" I think of as an attribute of the spirit. It is inward, and when we are fortunate, it sometimes affects us outwardly. I am certain of quietude in my spirit, even when outwardly I am disturbed, restless or anxious. I believe we were all born with this sanctuary within, this shelter. It is not indifference, or the shutting out of needs, our own and those of others.

As nearly as I can find words with which to clothe the wordless and translate it into ordinary terms, "quietude" is a sense of proportion, a consciousness of patience, a feeling of strength and purpose, and an acceptance of obedience; above all it is awareness of pure untarnished wonder. It is joy, which springs not from without but from within.

In my own personality, I am restless, talkative, unquiet, anxious. Quietude has nothing to do with personality, which is a matter of heredity and also of one's own manufacture. Perhaps quietude is a very slight revelation of Grace. I do not know. But that it is there, in each, for each to find, I am certain.

"How do you find it?" I am asked.

Your way may not be my way, and each must discover his own. Prayer is one way; not demands, not petitions, but prayer which goes out in love and pledges obedience. For obedience is also a Law, and part of the Law of Love. Who loves, and knows he is loved, will obey, even the willful child.

Winter, seen from within a warm room, is often physically quiet; snow makes no sound, and if there be no wind, the world about us seems to hold its breath. Spring is a restless season. The birds are busy, and growing things, although they make no sound, give us the impression that there is a stirring beneath the ground. We may be as restless as the nest-building bird, which goes from branch to branch and never seems to stay anywhere, and as forward-thrusting as the growing plants of spring, but we still can have the quietude which is silent as falling snow, yet as warm as sunlight.

And feel it around the clock of the year . . . every year.

❧ FIVE

April

APRIL MEANS EASTER TO MANY OF US, BUT ACTUALLY EASTER
Sunday, being a movable feast, can occur from late March
until late April. Whenever it comes, it is welcome as the
symbol of life's eternal resurrection.

I have known Easters as warm as June, others as cold as
some Februarys; a great many happy ones and some which
were not as happy. Who has not?

Thinking back over a number of Easters, I recall one
in the late nineteen twenties when I had a new gray flannel
suit and was determined to wear it and practically froze to
death riding top-coatless on a Fifth Avenue bus. And there
was another, sometime after 1936, when we took all the children to Atlantic City. Good Friday fell on March seventeenth
that year, and in front of our hotel the classic decorations,
which included many great containers of lilies, were frozen
black; and the lone, man-tall bunny, which presided over the

flowers, looked a little wan despite his plush coat; and when the pretty girls in their new hats went parading down the boardwalk their poor noses were red, white and blue.

In late March, if we are fortunate, forsythia spills its careless gold over wall and lawn and, where many bushes are planted together, it is brighter than sunlight. I often cut branches and force them, in the house, and they are a symbol and a precursor.

Under the big south window of the living room, the bulbs come up early, for they have full sun, and I look, long before it's time, for crocuses, yellow and purple, and often find April a steppingstone between March and May. It can be sullen, it can even snow; it can be warm as a good heart, but it's April anyway.

Writing about April and Easter, I think of the crucified Christ and the Risen. And last night I was thinking how comforting it is, how close it brings Him to us, to realize that He knew many of our human emotions. His was a righteous anger more than once. He could reproach gently, as well. He was happy to receive a gift lovingly, even extravagantly, bestowed. He prayed, as we all have done, that the cup might pass from Him, and in a moment of mortal pain and despair cried out to ask why His God had forsaken Him.

These are the qualities which bring us close to the Man, Himself, and which underline His understanding of our frailties.

For April, my birthday book is filled with notations. Practically everybody appears to have been born in April, I think, as I turn the pages: my sister, Esther; my twins, Ann and Stephen; my friend, Gladys Taber; my friend, Dorothy Olding. I have an April nephew, too. And upstate, where there is still snow in April, another friend; down on Long Island, a second cousin—and many more. And I never have enough birthday cards; just when I think I have laid in a stock, I find I am out of them. . . .

I must do some speaking this month, and I sometimes wonder why I do it. The trouble is I usually accept an invitation, if it's far enough ahead; I suppose I think the day will never come, but the first thing I know it has crept up and there it is, tomorrow, and I try to think what I am going to say. . . . I never do really, much more than ten minutes before the chairman of something or other has introduced me. . . . I must consider, the night before, what to wear and contrive how to get wherever I am going. Sometimes someone picks me up, as I don't drive; sometimes I go by taxi; often it's train or plane. . . . Once there, I always have a good time.

I, myself, am apt to sit uneasily during most speeches and my attention wanders. When my turn comes, I don't speak, I merely talk and digress, and wonder most of the time why in the world anyone has come to listen to me. I daresay they wonder, too, before many minutes have elapsed.

For many years I have worked for, and been connected with, an organization for child welfare, which is called Save the Children Federation, and for a short time I've sat at board and committee meetings. I wonder about this also. I don't often speak up, and when I do, it is with great misgiving, because at such discussions I always feel as if I were a child wearing my mother's garments and therefore present under false pretenses and with borrowed dignity. It is somewhat the same sensation I've had when, dressed in my best, I go into some elegant place, sit down at a table and immediately feel as if I were wearing a shawl and carrying a box lunch. I do not think this an inferiority complex or even a sense of insecurity. I believe it is simply a case of mild wonder: What am I doing here?

Save the Children Federation labors lovingly in many countries; it operates here in our own. I sponsor some children overseas, and here, a Navajo boy, none of whom I have been fortunate enough to meet. But I hear from them or their parents regularly. I have their pictures, too. I also sponsor a rural school in Kentucky. I went there once, some years ago to that school I sponsored. I traveled by plane and car, to creak finally along precipitous mountain roads and then walk up a big hill, or small mountain, in darkness, to see for the first time the one-room schoolhouse, the potbellied stove and the shy, silent children and parents.

Work with children in any field is rewarding. Early this winter I went to the Federation's annual board meeting—there are several board and committee meetings during the year, but this was the one preceding the award luncheon—and listened, not to speeches but to experiences, those of the organization's president and the program director, and, at a small committee meeting, to the illuminating words of the fine woman who directs the work in Greece. I looked at pictures which were like knives to stab the heart, listened to a recording, and at luncheon heard Lady Mountbatten accept the award for her work as head of the British Save the Children Fund. She did not make a speech but a warm, lovely offering of her heart.

Later, I talked to some of our area consultants in the mountain school regions; some I had met before; one was a good friend—and a miraculous driver, for he had brought me over those treacherous roads—and with some I had had personal contact through letters.

And all the time I thought about children.

Starving children, children without adequate clothing, children whose naked feet bleed scarlet on snow, children from sections of this country in which life is hard, and children from Europe and Asia whose homes have been destroyed by wars, poverty or illness; who have lost one parent or both; children who have stumbled across borders with their pitiful possessions; those to whom a doll or toy would seem unobtainable heaven, children who have never known what it is to be sufficiently housed or fed.

Adult needs are much the same as those of children. All of us need clothing, food and shelter, that much is certain; and there are innumerable grown people who suffer, as do the children, from lack of these. But there are deeper needs which are universal. The over-all needs of humanity are the same; some people are in better health than others; many do not have to take thought for the morrow as far as roof, bed and board are concerned; others have surplus money in their pockets and can buy all the toys which adults, also, desire. But the essential needs are love, security—which is primarily love—freedom and worship.

[83]

It is easy for the adult to understand the needs of children. If they are your own children, you will usually sacrifice anything in order to meet those needs; if they are not your own, you are nevertheless moved by their suffering and try to do something about it. But the heart of a child—even the richest child in the world, materially speaking—needs more than money can buy. And adults are all children, grown taller.

As the year wears on and I near the age at which we are told we can—under certain conditions—expect social security, I wonder about spiritual security.

Under the temporal law of social security, you and your employer each pay in a certain amount based upon your salary, and up to a given sum. If you are, as I am, self-employed, you make the entire deposit—also up to a limit. It seems somewhat complicated to anyone as unmathematical as I, yet even I understand it. But what about spiritual security?

That operates, I think, in much the same way except that, spiritually, we are always self-employed. No one pays in for or with me. We make our deposits ourselves from the time we are quite small until the day we die. Every day of every year we may add to the fund which can afford security. We do not have to wait until a stipulated age to draw upon it. As we daily pay, so also we can daily draw, from the great reserves of strength, hope and trust, from the enormous unfailing supply of God's love and patience, which is never exhausted.

But our payments must be in kind, in the human, faulty

way, for only then can we tap the ever-present reserve—love for love, patience for patience, understanding for understanding. And, as we must deal with human beings like ourselves, we are often called upon to pay in love, patience and understanding without, apparently, receiving them in return from those to whom we have given. But the unseen account books are closely kept, and in the long run we shall be repaid a thousandfold, as we look for and find the reserve in the strengthening of our spirits, the widening of comprehension, the deepening of patience. This too is a law.

I have a friend who recently said that other people might have spiritual resources, but she did not. It was in her case, she added, "hopeless."

She had put her finger on the cause in a single word— "hopeless." She was without hope, which is to say, without faith. She did not really believe in spiritual resources. She would not, or could not, be still and know. She is a charming, kind and gentle woman, beset, as we all are, with many difficulties. She was thinking outwardly and could not reach within to discover her own spirit, which she probably thinks of—if at all—as something apart from herself, having nothing to do with her. She did not stop to think that she *is* spirit, clothed in flesh.

When I write or speak of things of the spirit and of what I call Spiritual Law, I am unhappy afterwards, because I know that all I have produced is so many words, and what are words? Nothing you hear, and nothing you read, can prove Truth; you are compelled to prove it yourself. Someone may say, "Oh, I agree with you that there are spiritual laws, all stemming from the First Law of Love; justice is one, forgiveness, understanding, faith and joy, also." But even agreeing with it does not prove it.

A mathematician can prove an equation; at least he can prove it to most people, but not to me. I was born mathematically blind. I can barely add and subtract, and my brief struggle with algebra never convinced me that A plus B equals anything. Why should it? I am mildly certain that two and two make four, except in my checkbook where they make three or six, and in some departments of life in which nothing adds up to anything, or to far too much. . . . However, if you put two apples on my desk and add two more and I see them as apples, not as figures, I am fairly sure that once I had two apples and now have twice as many.

But you may be different and perhaps a mathematician can prove anything to you. Perhaps he can even prove something called "pi," which a friend of mine always disputes with her engineer husband. "Why?" she asks with great simplicity, and he can only reply that it has always been—pi.

Anyone can prove a physical truth. Even I can do that. If I put my hand on top of the range, with the burners on, I shall be scorched. If I fall out of a window, downstairs or off a ladder, I am almost certain to be battered and bruised or even to break a bone. If I can't swim, and walk into water over my head, I am likely to drown unless someone hauls me back to safety. If I eat something which disagrees with me, I shall regret it. And should I amble in front of a car or train, the result won't do me any good. Physical truths are easily proven even when we have no desire to be convinced of their validity.

But not so spiritual truths; to repeat them, to believe them, is fine, but it isn't "pi." For to prove them, you have to live them, and no one else can do that for you. I can tell you I have proven one or two a number of times, but that won't convince you. You have to convince yourself, and that is one do-it-yourself that no book can teach you.

For many years I believed many truths but, until proven through my own actions and reactions, I didn't *know* them. In other words two more apples had to be added.

St. Paul said in a frequently quoted passage that "all things work together for good." Most of us believe this until we stumble over obstacles and hurt ourselves, until disaster stuns and nothing appears to work together for anything save evil. Then we stop believing. The trouble is we didn't go on reading. St. Paul said "all things work together for good *to them that love God.*"

So the dismayed, unhappy person says, "But I have always loved God!"

There is still more, for St. Paul concluded, ". . . to them who are the called according to *His* purpose."

Who knows His purpose? Not until we have accepted it *without* knowing do we realize that there was a purpose and a plan, even in the obstacles and the disasters, and that we were, accordingly, called.

Yet if I say this to those who have not realized it, they will not believe me; nor will those who have so far gone through their days with apparently little or no difficulty.

One of the troubles with our times—and other times for that matter—is hurry . . . haste, impatience. "How wonderful," cries someone, leaping off a local subway and leaping onto an express. "I have saved three minutes." What does he intend to do with them, especially if he isn't en route to someone's sickbed, a vital appointment, a plane or train?

I often marvel at drivers on highways, cutting in and out, risking their own mortal lives as well as those of anyone near them. Usually, the car I am in catches up at the next intersection or light, and there is our weaver, sitting still. I wonder, too, about those who, driving behind us, lean upon their horns with passionate determination to hurry us, although the light may just be in the process of changing.

This has been going for years. We hurry when we talk, eat, or read, when we walk and even when we think. It bodes no good. When we talk in a hurry, we say nothing, or too much, before we know it; when we hurry at the table, we have discomfort thereafter; when we hasten through a book, we do not understand much that we read; and when we run instead of walking, we come to our destinations having seen nothing at all. As for hurrying when we think, we arrive nowhere or at the wrong decisions.

When I was a girl, and in Germany, I remember being in Hamburg the day after I arrived at Bremerhaven. Tante took me for a stroll, and I glanced at store windows as I went past. As far as I knew I was going along at a normal pace. But a woman stopped and smiled at me. She said, in English, "You're an American!"

I asked Tante, when she caught up with me, if Americans looked different from any other people and all she said was, "It was the way you were walking." I looked around me then and perceived that many people were on the street and that, while they appeared purposeful enough, none was in a hurry. They were walking past shops or under the trees by the river; they were enjoying an April day and none was out of breath.

As world tensions mount so do the tensions of the world's individual inhabitants. Half the people I know speak before they think because they are in such a hurry to get something said. We are in a rush to increase production, and, as the Western novels advocate, to beat everybody to the draw. I do not advise the snail's pace (although as I recall it, the tortoise won his race with the fleet-footed hare), or standing back, waiting for George to do it. A reasonable amount of concentrated effort is necessary in any household, business or government, but not the haste which ends in retracing one's steps.

There was once a surgeon—there still is—whom I consulted some sixteen years ago. He warned me, "If you want fast surgery, don't come to me. I take my time." He then stopped, smiled, and said, in his relaxed, quiet way (which afterwards I came to know very well), "But I don't have to go back and undo my work, or do it over again."

To do anything in life, large and small, in every department of it, I believe we were meant to take a reasonable length of time, and not to exhibit either unreasonable haste or unreasonable sloth. It took me so long to learn this. In fact, I haven't learned it entirely. I often find myself tearing through my mail or leaving a scant few minutes between this task and the next; going, sometimes literally, and sometimes figuratively, on the double. But sooner or later I remind myself to slow down, and the job gets itself done just the same.

Time was when, as a young writer, I worked against deadlines and produced an incredible amount of work at an equally incredible speed. Usually, it was because there was something immediate to be met . . . a crisis, a severe illness in the family. I have gone to hospitals by day, sometimes two of them, and worked at night, on little more than soup, and accomplished a good deal because my years were not many, my energy was tremendous, my vitality at the peak and my common sense at nadir.

An editor was once reported as saying, when someone failed him and he had what was known as a "hole" in the magazine, "Get Baldwin. She may be sloppy, but she's quick!"

That was the time I went out to California alone, by train, and on the way, wrote a novelette . . . while the much more eminent writer from whom a story had been expected was sitting quietly in Paris, not worrying. I was somewhat distressed by the "sloppy" but happy to get the chance. I daresay that any port in a storm, in those days, was an editorial must.

At that time I never rewrote anything except when editors screamed like stricken bunnies. Now I do rewrite, with infinite pains, and find to my sorrow that it rarely comes out much better. But, at least, I have taken the time to try.

Well, there's always today and tomorrow . . . and, as I have said, to learn to live a day at a time is the approach to peace. If we put into the gentle hands of God each today and each tomorrow, we will have found the worth of Seneca's words: "Begin at once to live and count each day as a separate life."

Just a while ago I looked at a snapshot of myself and my husband taken in the summer of 1922 at my father's farm. I had, to my recollection, never seen that picture before until it was sent to me by a friend of my young sister. She used to visit us and I would comb her long red hair while she howled in pain. This snapshot, much faded, came to me after my husband's death, and Barbara wrote she did not know why she had kept it, as she was not a person who saved things. But she had been at the farm that summer and we had appeared, to her young eyes, romantic in the extreme.

I have fixed the date because the snapshot shows trees in summer dress. In the summer of 1920 we were not yet married and besides, Hugh was in uniform. In 1921, we were in Puerto Rico, so this, and the fact that he is wearing hideous plus fours has enabled me to fix the time.

We are standing against a tree; there is a little bird cup for water on a tall rod beside us. I look at the snapshot many times. Who are these strangers? What became of them during the years? Yet there I am, although now scarcely discernible, and there he is, also. What were we thinking and feeling? How little, how much, did we know?

Actually, we all live a day at a time, and from day to day alter, looking back to find that, as we were yesterday, we are now. The same spirits prevail whatever happened to minds and bodies.

I have a deep affection for the clergy of all creeds. My closest friends, a clergyman and his wife, live not far from me, and it is he who has told me a number of things which I have put in my books. Another who has helped me is a Congregational clergyman at Storrs, where my younger son went to college. He and his wife are an inspiration. The clergyman who married my husband and me, and christened our children, was a Presbyterian, now gone beyond the narrow limits of this obstructed world. One of my friends, who left his earthly post while I was in London in 1954, was a Jesuit priest and very old at the time of his departure. Another, also of the Society of Jesus, is young and a professor in a California college. . . . I live next door to nursing Sisters of a fine, sacrificial order; and the acres beyond them belong to the Holy Ghost Fathers, who are wonderful neighbors. Not long since, Father Walsh, who heads the seminary which trains young men for missionary service in Africa, gave me a biography of the man who founded their Order —a Jew, who, like Saul of Tarsus, became a Christian. From Oklahoma and Texas a teaching Sister has written me for years; in the Philippines I have many friends, of various creeds; and from Maryland, Father Gilbert and I keep in touch. He heads the Trinity Missions there—a group of missionary priests who serve in our own country.

The woman who helped me with "American Family," my book on China, was born of Methodist missionaries in China; her people knew mine; her husband came of a family in missionary service in India. They married and went to China; they are now, as far as I know, in Burma. . . .

I corresponded for a long time with a great rabbi, Joshua Loth Liebman, whose book, *Peace of Mind,* brought so much to so many; and I greatly mourned his early death. My father's house was always open to those who worked in whatever religious field was theirs; through him I knew Rabbi Wise, Doctor Cadman and Cardinal Farley.

Anyone who has ever come in contact with the devoted servants of God can have only love and respect for each. All creeds have their differences; the Roman Catholic Church is not the only Catholic Church, and Protestants have as many sects as there are buds on an April bush. Judaism differs three ways. And, I daresay, those who are of Islam, or who follow Hindu creeds or Buddhism, also differ. It doesn't matter.

I have been in cathedrals, chapels and meeting houses. I have, on entering temples, removed my shoes. Wherever a structure rises, dedicated to God, there He is. If we respect one another, we have taken the first essential step upon the road of Brotherhood. For, who loves God, in whatever guise and through whatever form, loves the God of all men, all religions, creeds, races and colors.

Only by chance am I not a Negro or an American Indian . . . as are many of my friends. I was not born an Asian in the far or the near East. I wasn't born in Europe either.

I just happened to be born in the United States, and the creed in which I was raised was ancestral.

It is but a happen-chance that I am what I am, as far as race and birthplace go. This is true of all. There are many conversions from one creed to another, but the converts are outnumbered by those who remain with the creed of their parents.

As I said, in the dedication of another book to a Moslem, "All roads lead to God." It was he who taught me this.

Just now I looked up, my eyes being tired from typing, and saw the pictures near me: the photograph of Li Hung-chang; an etching, done by a gifted friend, of Edgar Allan Poe; and the steel engraving of Abraham Lincoln which used to hang over my father's desk. How diversified these men, their earthly lives, and the conclusions thereof. The great Prime Minister of a fabulous Empress; the bewildered, unhappy genius; the compassionate, humorous Kentuckian who went to Illinois and became a lawyer. We all know that Lincoln was deeply religious and that his belief in guidance was rooted. I have no idea what Li Hung-chang's religion was. I know only of the record of his statesmanship, which is not unblemished. But if he worshipped his ancestors, he must have known of the original ancestry of all men. And Poe believed . . . if never himself.

For a long time now there has been an urge publicly to overthrow mortal heroes. We used to call it "debunking." It may be all right to expose frailties, if not to ridicule them, but there should be a balance between ruthless judgment and legend. Those of us who have not—and never will—

become heroic figures feel less inferior when we read that an eminent person was not perfect. Yet who knows the absolute truth about anyone, including himself? Man, in hardship, has discovered vast territories of land, sailed unfriendly seas, climbed tremendous mountains, yet how little is known about one man, any man.

Psychiatrists seek to explore the region of man's mind. They have learned much; but not everything. And few take into consideration the spirit—even if they are able to explore it.

Many of us, having been born to or having found our path, cannot go along with the dogmas, tenets, ideologies and theologies of the neighbor who is on his different road. So be it. But we can go along with the effort of his spirit. I cannot say, or think, often enough that in order to live peacefully in this world, one must recognize respect for one's fellow man as a basic spiritual law.

For all men spring returns sometime, whether in their country it be in April or in another month; for all there is the resurrection of life and the pouring out of the sun. Do you believe that God made the spring to blossom for a few, or that His love is confined to those of one creed or another? I am sure you do not. And if you do not, then that is a truth which you have proven to yourself.

Always the Risen Life, the promise and the hope. For you, for me, for everyone, this little world over, forever.

May

MAY IS A GENTLE MONTH. THE DIFFICULTIES AND UNEXPECTED punitive measures of March are forgotten, together with April's willful ways. May also has her moods; she can blow both hot and cold but is, primarily, a month of growth and budding effort, a month of birds—my orioles always return in May and streak past the windows like animated tulips. And always the established spring brings an up-welling of hope.

As May goes, free blooming, all about us, I sometimes occupy myself in meditative remembering, for it is a memorial month. . . . Just now I stopped to wind my mother's clock. It runs for eight days and then collapses with the most dreadful sighs, groans and crashes.

I've had it for some years. It's a wall clock, with a pendulum, and pretty, in a faded, flower-decorated green. It's old but not very old, and I am the only one who winds it. Those who help me here are slightly and mistakenly superstitious about it; they believe it won't go for anyone but me, so when I am away it runs down and remains silent until my return. Actually there is no magic about it. You wind it with a key, and you see that it is level on the wall. This is the trick, for the walls are old and sometimes the clock looks level but isn't. So it ticks awhile with a loud, positive voice, which grows weaker and then ceases altogether. I have often wound it in haste, started the pendulum swinging and sat down, only to have it stop. On such occasions I've been alone, so the family hasn't discovered that I don't always know the formula. I have had to rise three or four times with muttered words of annoyance before the exact level, the right balance was achieved.

That is like most things, isn't it? To attain a smooth, constant running of your life, you have to find the balance and the level.

Some of my mother's jewelry came to me not long ago, and I sent most of it to my girls who are young enough to enjoy it. But I kept two things.

One is a little gold hairpin, on the top of which there is a pearl. I often saw it in her beautiful hair, and I pin it in my own now. And when people discover it, they look at me with amazement. A gray curl above my forehead with a pearl in it! It is, somehow, a more intimate trinket than a ring or a brooch. Yet, I kept one ring. I never saw my mother wear it, and I can't imagine where she obtained it or why. It isn't her type of ring at all.

It is a Chinese ring. Perhaps someone in my father's

family brought it to her or gave it to her out of a family jewel box. Perhaps she bought it in San Francisco. It is a silver ring, with flowers carved around the setting. The stone is an amethyst carved with a flower, a darker streak running through it. It is a simple ring, not intrinsically valuable.

But I think of the man who carved it, sitting in the back of his shop or in his home, painstakingly making an amethyst flower and working with silver; concentrated upon his work, which was creative, for all craftsmen, no matter with what substance they labor, are creative artists. Perhaps it took quite a long time, during which people came and went and he didn't notice. Perhaps a wife or daughter brought him his tea or his rice, and he nodded and went on working. This is why I wear the ring, not only because the color appeals to me but because into it went something of a man's life and creative talent. It is the color of Maytime, of the lighter violets with a streak of the darker; and of the silver slice of a moon.

But the ring is equally at home in winter after a spectacular cold-weather sunset when the brightness fades and the sky is swept with the muted colors which follow the sun's sinking; in a winter sunset there's a green you don't see at any other time and a pink mauve which sometimes deepens into violet.

I have a great attachment to Chinese things. I have often written of my small collection of Kwan Yins, some very old; of the Imperial china rice bowls and plates; of ivories and cloisonné and prints; of the snuff bottles, eggshell jars and ginger jars, and probably about the curious wine ewer and the rice-grain porcelain bowls, cups and saucers.

There are boxes, too—I gave one away this morning —and the miniature slipper my missionary grandmother took from the cruelly bound feet of a young woman. I once had a bracelet of softest gold, set with jade, brought to me by a friend. I have since given it to my daughter-in-law, Janet; my given name is on it, in Chinese.

Kwan Yin in wood—she was fashioned in my father's birthplace—looks at me from the mantel as I write. She was a gift. I rarely buy anything Chinese. My first Kwan Yin—which is possibly Japanese, and which lives in a tiny shrine with closing doors—I did buy, walking into a shop in Washington, discovering the owner had been brought up by missionary parents in the same compound as my father. He later sent me an invitation to a birthday party for Father which, all those years, he had preserved. But most of my Oriental things came from missionary friends, from my family, or more recently from Chinese friends in this country.

Some years ago I was given a Chinese puzzle ball. This one rests in a little scooped-out piece of ivory, attached to a slender rod, which is balanced by the ivory figure of a man. I often lift the ball from its resting place and turn it over in my hands, for it is delicately carved in intricate patterns. Also, it contains, one within the other, many such balls . . . there are, in all, ten concentric spheres.

My friends wrote that they were told in Canton years ago that the puzzle balls are made by following this general rule: a crude ball of solid ivory is first pierced in several directions through the center and then divided into spheres by means of cutting tools, with stops on the handles, introduced into the holes. These spheres are, in turn, revolved, to be cut into openwork of various patterns. The task is most tedious and exacting, and a tiny error could nullify the labor of many weeks and months. My friends added that such work, which is one of the wonders of Chinese ingenuity and patience, is highly regarded, as producing treasures of beauty and rarity unsurpassed by other craftsmen of the world.

Someone else said that many who did this work—and I doubt it is being done now—lose their eyesight. I wish he hadn't told me that.

When first I received the puzzle ball, I would hold and admire it, and try to count the little spheres as I revolved it in my hand. I would think of my grandparents, so long in China, and of my father. But lately I have begun to think of this ivory puzzle as symbolic.

The other day, sitting in the big chair by the east window, looking through the mulberry branches, down the slope past the maples, apple trees and dogwoods, to the pond where duck and pheasant come for their pan of grain, I glanced over at the desk by the window, on which the ivory man balances the spheres, and found myself thinking of it as a symbol of human life and spirit.

I thought: So we begin as a single, crude but valuable solid, and so we form ourselves as the years pass, sphere within sphere, according to our thoughts and acts, and the choices we make.

No one, looking from outside, sees all the spheres wholly; just the outside one, and glimpses of the inner.

Of course no two people are exactly alike, mentally or physically, and factors of hereditary strength and weakness enter in. My analogy may be generalized but, is, I believe, true in the main. Let us put it this way—what we are originally given, we personally shape.

As we grow, the original shape is truly pierced in several directions and into our hands the cutting tools are placed. Circumstance and environment are, of course, directions, but I think each can be overcome, if bad, or taken advantage of if good. And there are so many tools with which to cut the patterns. Ambition can make a wonderful sphere within a sphere, provided the tool follows a spiritual direction and does not become ambition at the sacrifice of something more valuable. Adversity is a keen-edged tool; pain another, and so is grief. Happiness is a tool which can be used to make a lovely pattern, but lovelier are cut by compassion. Love is, of course, the greatest, surest tool of all, in any form and relationship, but selfless love is the most difficult tool to come by . . . you have to make *that* tool yourself.

Here, too, a tiny error in judgment, in justice, in direction and path selection can certainly nullify the work of many weeks—or years.

But one difference between the Chinese artist's block of solid ivory and the malleable stuff of the human spirit

is that the tools with which to rectify errors are always in our hands. I suppose that, if the ivory-carver makes a really serious mistake, he must cast aside his material and begin again. But our material is never cast aside nor lost. We make a mistake, then learn to rectify it. In this way character is built, patterned over the years, and reflected in the growth of the spirit.

I have always found it unrewarding to become complacent or smug. I have been—most of us have, now and then—but I don't like the fat, chop-licking feeling it gives me. I am constantly aware of the fact that, however much I try to be a "good child," I fail. The best I can do is try again. This sense of failure is another tool, but unless it is used with its partner, the will to try again, it is destructive in the extreme.

Sometimes I am distressed by the fact that zealous strangers want to "reform" me. They don't agree with some of my ideas, opinions or thoughts, with what I write, with the way (they fancy) I live. They haven't a clear idea of what I think except as revealed in articles like these, and even here I do not fully express myself. No one can, for no one really knows himself or his motives completely; thoughts and opinions are apt to be surface matters.

No stranger knows how I live, or by what code. Some are upset because they chance upon my fiction writing and find it "worldly." I have never claimed to be other than of this world. Some believe that every sentence I write into the mouth of a character in a story must stem from my own experience; every opinion must be my own. If such readers

would stop to think that I have written about seventy books and innumerable short stories, they would realize that I could not possibly agree with everything thought and expressed by heroes, heroines, villains and minor characters. The writer of fiction endeavors to make his characters conform to what he believes to be their patterns of thinking and behavior.

In one of my earliest novels there was some discussion of the First World War, and a character in the book referred to the enemy of that period as a "Hun" (a popular word at the time). I later had a letter from an older friend whom I most dearly loved; during part of that war I had lived with her in Germany. She was half English, half German, and wholly torn. I had gone to Europe to travel with her, but we were caught and held in Germany until passports came through and various intricate matters were settled. I had many friends there and had been shown much kindness. I was young and it was exciting, though horrible, for I had little understanding of war. Now, she reproached me in her letter for the use of the word "Hun."

But I didn't use it. My character did. He would have done so in that day, age, time and circumstance.

It is hard to make people realize this.

Yet, if I decided that a man in a story should desire to murder his brother and said so, would any reader believe that I had a lurking desire to murder my brother, provided I had a brother (which I haven't)?

I have caused fiction characters to do and say a great many things I wouldn't do or say. I have also made them do many fine things I myself would never have the necessary nobility or intelligence to accomplish.

I am sure that people do not understand all this, so I do not get angry, upset or perturbed. I know why *they* write as they do.

Attacks on my personal life are something else again, and I am still groping to reach a haven of tranquillity there. The best I can do is not to retaliate. Like everyone else, I have read in the papers something about a total stranger which affronted me, and have instantly condemned him or her in my mind. So, I don't do it any more; at least I try not to. This all boils down to what I have often said. At the risk of being repetitious I say it again. I don't think it can be said too often or thought about too much:

How do you—how do I—know what motivates anyone? What do you know of others' heredity, upbringing or environment, of their struggles and sorrows, of their unhappiness and hurts?

The "reformers" mean well, but somehow I don't think their efforts will be greatly counted in their favor. Large issues, yes, those which embrace mankind's progress, salvation, hope—the tremendous battles which come under the head of reform, which deal with wars, with inequities, with mercy, with the overcoming of poverty, hopelessness, disease. But not the petty effort to set one's neighbor straight, whether he be friend or stranger. There was a Man who said, "Thou shalt love thy neighbour as thyself," and also advised that the beam in one's own eye be cast out before one attempts to remove the mote from another's.

I often pray that I may be able to cast out my own beam, but I am afraid that I do not, as often, make the necessary effort.

None of us wholly approves of everything other people do. We don't find the décor of their house to our taste; we haven't their allergies, we have our own; we like red meat, and they are vegetarians or vice versa. Sometimes we don't approve of the way in which others bring up their children, and I have yet to find anyone who agrees with the way anyone else saves or spends money. One man's string saving offsets his expensive car. Someone else uses subways instead of taxis, but goes to Europe once a year. Few see eye to eye on budgets, extravagances, thriftiness.

We don't approve of each other's choice in wives or husbands. We say, "My dear, what did she see in him?" or "What did he see in her?" We think people are in the wrong jobs. We give advice only to find that most people, even if they ask for it, don't want it; they just wish to be told that what they want to do is what they should do. If friends live in town and we live in the country, we don't approve of their living in town, and never stop to think that lots of people *like* the city and would be miserable in the country!

Someone is bound to write me that he or she can also quote the Bible, and I shall be told that I am my brother's keeper. But perhaps we read a different meaning into the great words. I am, indeed—in compassion and in love—but I do not believe that I have been told to be his keeper in the sense of putting him in bondage to my ideas.

If I were asked what spiritual gift I most desire, I would put one above all: the gift of impersonal love. Impersonal, in the sense that it would flow out to every living creature and under any conditions. I would ask—and I do —that I be given the ability to see the spirit of God in every human being I encounter, however adversely these persons affect me, however differing their opinions, however repellent their natures to me, or however incompatible the way in which we live our lives. I shall not achieve this. I doubt if this is given to any of us, wholly. It is an attribute of God. We can only ask, aspire, try and try again.

So we come back to the concentric spheres. The way we view our fellow man is another tool, and one which slips easily, and, in the slipping, harms our own pattern.

Motive is a tool with which we also cut patterns . . . a good one, a bad one, or in a sense, no motive at all. . . . I have always questioned my own and was told once to stop worrying, for no amount of soul-searching would give the answer except to what was outward and recognized.

Motivation is something fiction editors are always talking about. "But, where," they ask, "is the *motivation?*"

A few days ago I had occasion to read two short stories written by the friend of a friend. I am not much of a critic —if I were I would never write another line—but I tried to use the editorial yard stick. So, of course, I came up with the querulous question which has so often chilled me to the marrow. "But, where's your motivation?" When I had said it, I laughed inwardly. For I remembered thinking years ago, that many wrote mystery stories, so why couldn't I? I soon had a wonderful plot sketched out, even to the weapons which were unusually genteel, a knitting needle for one. I read my notes, somewhat later, and realized that there was no motive at all for murder, not the frailest. There was no reason whatsoever for the two poor creatures in the story neatly to be skewered. I tossed the notebook away.

Sometimes when we do what others—and perhaps, secretly, ourselves—consider good and later examine the motive, we are horrified.

If we fashion a crutch for someone, he may use it all his life. If we show him how to walk without it, crippled though he is, he may overcome his handicap. Many parents have forever crippled their children by an oversupply of "crutches."

The clergyman who told me about looking view-ward told me another story. He said that a woman he hadn't seen for some time came to him to say that something had happened to her, that she now realized many of her attitudes had been wrong. This amazed him, for he had thought of her always as a person who sacrificed herself for others.

This he said, and she replied that, yes, indeed, she had spent most of her adult life overflowing with kindness. In the office where she worked she was always telling someone to run along, she'd finish the job. She used her free time to dispense bounty; she did good deeds, visited the ill, and gave of her earnings. She said she could not call her soul her own. But, suddenly, she discovered that her soul *was* her own. None possessed it except herself—through God, from God.

She said, in effect, "All I have done for people has been from sentimentality. When I did other people's work for them, it was wrong. They should have done it themselves, and maybe wanted to, but I always insisted. Often I spent a day at a friend's bedside, when perhaps she would have preferred to be alone. When I gave money carelessly, I was encouraging people not to earn. Now I find I can follow the dictates of a more rational principle. I can give to those truly in need, not as a sedative, or a lollipop, and never as a permanent crutch, but as a temporary arm beneath the elbow, helping over a specific obstacle. Many people used what I gave them as a crutch. They should have been encouraged to stand upon their own feet. But I was sentimental."

Now her life had altered for the better. She found herself free to enjoy it. She was not continually fretting about people for whom her impulse toward careless kindness was more detriment than help. She was learning to be selective and to follow the dictates of reason rather than unthinking generosity.

I was interested in this, for I had found, over a number of years, that much of what I had done for others had sprung also from sentimentality and sometimes from vanity. If friends decided they needed a certain amount of money, I gave it, not always being able to spare it but managing to do so because I did not want anyone—least of all my temporarily embarrassed friends—to know that I, too, was temporarily embarrassed. This motivation was sheer vanity or something equally deplorable.

Motivation is a curious thing and most of us do not know our own motives. I have no doubt that my clergyman's friend did many things which later proved to be for good; perhaps I, too, have accomplished this. But I believe that sentimentality (which is not sentiment) is selfish, and vanity certainly is.

How many times have we been asked for a charitable donation and, not really able to afford it, have given it because the amount will be made public and we feel that ours should be as much, if not more, than the next person's? This is not a sincere offering, but a giving to enhance our own prestige in the eyes of other people.

Awareness of this attitude influences those who ask for donations. They come and, in effect, say, "Mr. Davis has given so much. I know you are in a better position, and I therefore assume that you will give more than he did."

Few of us have the courage to say flatly, "I cannot afford *that* much, but I can afford *this*, and I will give it freely and with love."

How often do we go out of our way to do for others because we feel they are in some measure superior to us, either by ancestry, money, intelligence, education or achievement? It makes us feel superior, for the moment, to believe we have done a favor for someone usually better able to do one for us.

Purity of purpose, spontaneous outgoing, lack of selfish

motivation are, I think, impossible wholly to achieve. But if we achieve only a little, how much inner happiness it brings. The complete lack of desire for reward is perhaps the first step. This does not mean that whatever we have to give, whether in substance, advice or service, should be carelessly bestowed. Which brings us right back to sentimentality and vanity.

A man should have pride, not vanity. The kind of pride I mean is self-respect. God-made, one must have it in order to live on amiable terms with oneself, to develop that self according to the law and justice of God.

There is an ancient Chinese ceremonial called *kowtow*, which consists of abasing oneself to the knees and knocking one's head against the floor.

I believe that this old word can be used to describe attitudes of the spirit as well as those of the outer consciousness. We can reasonably kowtow before the person who has attained real power—not of money, not even of mental achievement alone, but power of spirit.

In our own spirits the kowtow is the attitude of humility toward the wonder of life and the Supreme Power which gave it to us. It is, so to speak, a God-ward effort. It is not just prayer; it is something with which we daily live, a humble, lowly road upon which to travel.

As spring comes, the spirit within man consciously or unconsciously makes this prostration before the Power which moves bountifully through the world, ordaining the seasons; bringing to all the passing of winter, the cessation of cold rains and darkness; shining forth in beauty and resurrection of growth. No one living on this earth and experiencing these wonders can fail to see the working of God's plan in the coming of the spring. And to this the spirit within man must bow.

The paradox is that, only when we inwardly kneel, can we also stand erect and move forward. All life is progression, here and hereafter; nothing remains static; none can, for long, mark time. For move we must, and even if the direction changes, we are still moving as God wills.

To know this gives us assurance. It is as simple as effective prayer. For we can pray, silently or aloud, for hours on end and yet not reach the awareness of acceptance, and knowledge of guidance contained in four short words, "Thy will be done."

Not yours, not mine, but His.

It takes a while to learn this.

May is a fine month, wet or dry. I always welcome the season's change, as I do the change in my own house from winter to spring trappings. And I like four seasons though many do not. Most of my friends wish for a perpetual summer or spring; some would live forever in the sunny, cool days of autumn. But I like contrasts.

I recognize that life itself is largely contrast, though it also possesses qualities which are not seasonal but year-round, year-long, life-long: courage and kindness, trust and gratitude, the rising above despair, the desire to be humble, the ability to feel compassion.

These, we try to acquire in the school of the spirit

where each in his own way learns to live, to pray, and to know there is one gift which we daily receive, and which in order to receive we must give. That gift is love. And we keep only what we give.

Losing is not giving, yet sometimes when we lose, we gain, and in defeat are victors. Remember Jesus said, "he that loseth his life for my sake . . . shall find it"? I think of another interpretation of "losing one's life for His sake," and that is: only if a man lose *himself* can he know himself and be the gainer. For Self can become anything from a tyrant to a slave, from a murderer in a spiritual sense, to a burden. To lose oneself in selflessness is something few accomplish, but there the smallest loss is gain.

Whatever happens, or doesn't, there is love; love from God, from those close to us, from friend and stranger. Love is not for the springtime season alone. Love is for always.

With the oriole returning to weave his intricate dwelling far above the greening earth, and the brook overbrimming its boundaries, there is hope. No matter what havoc we have made, what tests we have failed or passed, no matter how often we have abused our privileges and stumbled upon the path, there is always above and about us the unfailing love, bounty and understanding, the forgiveness and enfolding of the Divine Intelligence to Whom we speak, saying, in humility—"Our Father . . ."

SEVEN

June

JUNE IS AS CAPRICIOUS AS A WOMAN. WE THINK OF APRIL IN terms of charming clichés—laughter, tears; and of May as soft and biddable, faithful to her promise. But who regards June as whimsical and willful?

I do.

One tenth of May it was so warm that walking home, two blocks from the church where my little sister's wedding had taken place, I melted, like a wedding luncheon ice, on the pavement. Yet, twenty-two days later, when my husband and I were in the country, it was so cold that we started the furnace and lighted hearth fires. It was, also, very wet. June can blow hot or cold; wet or dry. She has her own ideas.

Two years ago I planned an early evening barbecue for a group of women belonging to a business and professional club of which I was an honorary member. All was in readiness on that June Saturday—the outdoor tables, the grille. . . .

I have never seen it rain harder or longer.

However her whims may afflict us, June is a month dedicated to commencements, brides, the beginning of vacations, sentiment and joy.

I love her. I can take July and August in my stride and let them depart, but there is something about June which motivates me to seize her by her green-gold skirts and say, "Linger."

She doesn't. She goes her appointed way, as does everything.

This past year, we have experienced a difficulty in the economy of the nation. For a long time, we rode the high crest of the wave, but in all things there is also a low and a middle trough.

I recall a real depression and the bank closings. Fortunately, I had a small amount of emergency cash—in a wall safe; this took care of the grocer, the butcher and the druggist, who, good friends, would have trusted me anyway. Also, I was moved successfully to write a series of novelettes which reflected the immediate times. They were afterwards put into a book which dealt exclusively with the happenings of one year.

I remember bread lines.

This is a country which goes up on the wave and down, but always finds its true level. I believe in it, and so do you. When lean times come and sacrifices are demanded, the American people—who, during good times are gay, casual and critical—cinch their belts and discover their neighbors. People are always discovering neighbors, as in the First

World War, the depression and World War Two. Those who had lived near one another for years and said no more than "good morning" and "good evening" because their circumstances or tastes differed, learned about common denominators. All who had sons of suitable age saw them go to war; many did not return.

Nothing welds the American—and other—people as closely as mutual danger, disaster and anxiety. Is it not wonderful? Is it not tragic? Wonderful because in bad times this happens; tragic because in good times it does not?

Prior to the Second World War we moved to a country community and became acquainted with a number of pleasant people. After Pearl Harbor there was not sufficient gasoline to power social activities. What we were permitted, we conserved, and so, saw only those who had truly become our friends, were willing to expend rationed fuel in order to be with us. We did not see those who had once been happy to come to our parties, sit around our swimming pool or invite us to theirs.

In that conflict, I had considerable stake: two sons, three nephews, the sons of many friends, the husbands of friends younger than I. So I went to work, employing the only weapon at my command—which was a typewriter—to write more articles about the American way of life, which were translated and sent world round, more slogans and appeals than I can count. I also used my voice in public speaking and recorded it in German, so that what I said could be transmitted by radio through the O.W.I. to receivers which were forbidden in Germany but to which many people, silently and fearfully, listened. And I remember another broadcast, which, translated into Norwegian, went to men manning the brave ships of Norway upon the dangerous seas.

In those days we lived for the censored broadcasts, the newspapers and the letters.

Early in 1942 a surgeon said to me that every man in his time lives through two—or possibly three—major wars. I could concede this. World War One was my young war; and the second, my older. But I can recall personal repercussions of a war in which Theodore Roosevelt and his Rough Riders stormed San Juan Hill. I was a child and knew nothing except that my father's best friend, returning from the Spanish American conflict, sat, in midsummer, by a round hot stove in our Cape Cod cottage when the chills of malaria overtook him.

I knew of the Russo-Japanese war mainly from overhearing the conversation of my elders, and much later from a great man in the theater, whom I well knew and loved, and whose Japanese manservant, when reading the newspapers, had made comments that his employer never forgot.

The Balkan Wars, the Chinese-Japanese War—all these were in my lifetime. Always the distant, flaring fires.

I once believed that the world moved in peace, with intervals of war. I know now that, for centuries, it has moved in war with intervals of peace.

When I was a girl, I was caught in Germany because a war was on. My father, at home, was sure it would be short, and he was afraid of travel for me, because of submarines.

Besides, there was no money available for me from America. A German bank carried my mother's friend with whom I was living, my parents having planned that I should travel with her all over Europe. I have spoken of her before. I called her Tante. I was in Germany from April, 1914, to April two years later. All this was before the United States entered the war; and I saw only German newspapers, only German people and their allies—I particularly remember the Turkish officers; those I met were as handsome and romantic as any fairy-tale princes—and I did volunteer work in German hospitals. All I saw there was suffering.

Anyone who sees any war, no matter where he is, must see suffering; also deprivation and courage. And, looking closer, avarice, and people who make capital out of other people's needs.

On any side of the curtain, this is true, as is the impact on any people, any home, anywhere.

My ancestors fought in what is called the Revolution. I don't know about those who lived during the War of 1812. In the War Between the States some of my blood were on each side; others, being Quakers, did not fight at all. A young uncle of mine ran away from school to fight in Cuba; my parents' friends were in the war with Mexico. My husband, and many of my friends and relatives, fought in the First World War . . . I have told you my stake in the Second. So in a lifetime, which is short or long, according to the way you regard it, I have seen wars. And gone through one dark depression without knowing it, and another which I knew very well. I have experienced rationing without real hardship and seen in our country kitchen the produce of our own acres being canned for our table, other tables and the kitchen of the community school.

But everything passes.

On the battlefields, many survive and many do not; and many go home to what is a part-time survival. In many countries the home front has been almost as perilous as the battle front; so far ours has not been. There were black markets, the world around. There were people everywhere who grumbled at lack . . . and usually found supply. Most of us here were cheerful enough, even without inexhaustible sugar, meat, coffee, gasoline.

When we pray for our country and its leaders, past politics—did not Abraham Lincoln say of an opponent that he "put country above party"?—we should also pray for all countries. When we pray that our leaders be given spiritual wisdom and guidance, should we not ask it for all who bear the physical burden of responsibility and decision, omitting neither the apparently good nor the apparently evil?

There was One who told us to pray for our enemies. We are often reluctant to do this, but if we look back, we sometimes see that yesterday's enemy has become today's ally.

To pray for one's enemy is to disarm him, spiritually speaking, whether he is a personal or an impersonal foe. God grant that he also prays for us, *his* enemy.

Let us not be afraid. Man-devised moons soar into space, but the ancient, un-manufactured moon is still there. Man seeks to invade the natural moon. I wonder why? Who shall conquer the myriad stars and planets and to what purpose? There is space beyond the comprehension of the greatest scientific mind, and on any night the stars in their courses obey a natural law; the moon rises, waxes, or wanes. This has obtained always, long before man crept out from caves and dared to lift his eyes skyward; and will obtain always, whether or not man in his folly has destroyed himself.

I have said, quoting a Book, "Be still and know." No matter what destruction is loosed, what despair, no matter what weapons rage in a shrinking world, the skies remain, the stars are there. The contemplation of infinity, plan and purpose quiets the mind and heart.

The world is as it has ever been since that same caveman emerged cautiously to attack a man in a cave half a mile distant. That, basically, history repeats itself there can be no doubt. Man arms for war over ideologies, divisions of opinion, and religion. To what have "religious" wars led? To the torture of Jews, the murder of Catholics, the slaying of Moslems, the destruction of Protestants. I am convinced that in any war God is neutral, and I ponder His compassionate sorrow when He contemplates what man has wrought.

Wars differ in weapons—longer range, more deadly—as time advances; yet, it is not such a far cry from boiling oil poured from a parapet, flaming arrows and battering rams to the hydrogen bomb. Wars differ in strategy and cunning. Once they were fought from the caparisoned backs of horses; once there were swords clashing on armor . . . later the trench, the foxhole and the radio.

Navies have battled, moved under the oars of galleys,

under sail, steam and oil. I can remember when submarines first poked their long noses above water. Now a submarine can travel, in silence, across an ocean, without refueling.

Wars in the air are younger than I. Once I flew in what had been, not long before, a Navy plane. It was built like a chicken crate. I sat in an open cockpit, on a hot spring day, as we flew above the water around Key West. I wore a leather helmet, and had been told, before I clambered in, to remove my hair pins lest they fly free and damage a propeller. Nothing before had ever been as exciting as that flight, I thought; and certainly nothing was ever as noisy. If I had been about to faint, I could not have made the pilot, sitting next to me, hear.

As wars erupt, are waged and ended, the economic barometers of nations rise and fall. Countries grow fat with prosperity, and careless. They lose economic weight and become lean; then put on weight again.

I am not afraid. Are you?

Our country, which is as a child among older nations, is a strong child, often willful and demanding, sometimes badly mistaken, but always strong. It will grow. Yet it is not as young as Australia and New Zealand, and the way they have grown, since I first saw them in 1939, is past belief. I returned, in 1954, to see for myself their strength and forward-going. We are not as young as our neighbor, Canada, and have seen her grow also. And there have been new births among divided and merging nations. More than one this very year.

Policies, politics and pressures, the shifting of the balance of power—these have been with us since the beginning of civilization. Nations, greater in their time than ours or any other, have flourished, fallen and risen again, if not to the positions they once held, still, to position.

Depressions are not unusual. There was a bad one here in the 'seventies, and another shortly after I opened uncomprehending eyes upon this world. My father, even then a brilliant, successful lawyer, broke open my china bank and took its contents for a grocery bill. He told me about it eighteen years later when, having computed the compounded interest, he opened my first checking account for me. He was a man who always paid his debts.

I am not fearful. Having survived close to sixty-five years, I shall continue to survive for as long as God wills, whether in this house, another, or no house at all. What does it matter?

People, latterly, have become fearful again, and fear begets fear. Of what are they afraid? The answer is apparent: they are afraid generally, not so much for themselves as for the lives of their sons and grandsons. They are afraid, if less immediately, of ration lines and empty cupboards; but more of telegrams from a war office.

We as a people have taken all this before, but never for the long years the British endured it.

Someone spoke to me the other day of 1929, when men, highly regarded in financial circles and doubtless much loved by their families, leaped from high windows or set loaded guns to their heads. Now and then, one still does.

Almost everyone, a year earlier, had been rich on paper:

the butcher, the baker, the candlestick maker; the man next door and the one round the corner; the captain, the waiter and the bus boy.

Many lost what they had never had.

I often think of the impassioned prayer which has gone upwards, like candle smoke, during every war the world has known. In those I have known clergymen of every creed and language have prayed that their side emerge victorious. Other people prayed for their own.

God takes no sides. The enemy's son is as dear to Him as ours . . . our sons are the enemy's enemies. Why should we believe that the Creator identifies by uniform? Man has free will. Usually, he says the war he wages is idealistic, and sometimes, in conception, it is. But profoundly there is the desire to conquer, to become the most powerful; and much is born of greed. However idealistic in theory, it is because of greed and the power complex that wars are waged. Yet all sides proclaim that theirs is the righteous war.

Man is free to do his own will. God waits.

We are not here for long. Let us make the most of it. Live fully, and living, learn; and fear not.

It is impossible never to be anxious for those we love, and each of us needs, and asks for, his daily bread. Ask then, for sufficiency, and beyond that, do not fear.

Physical fearlessness is not courage. A human body which cannot experience pain is unconscious or the nerves are dead. A man without physical fear is one who lacks some vital nerve. The brave man fears, yet goes forward. For moral courage is not physical courage.

Trust is easily shaken; belief in someone close, or in a position, bank account, friend, or theory. Faith is not shaken, nor is spiritual knowledge.

I have faith in discipline. It is a hard-sounding word, and we see fashions in child guidance rise, fall and return again. Psychologists dissect, weigh and make pronouncements— some for discipline and some against. Do not say, "No." Never say, "You must not." Appeal to the reason, divert the attention. Fine! But diversion can be carried a little too far, if, for instance, you take away a gun and substitute a knife.

Always, I believe, a child is happier under discipline, if it be wise, understanding and loving. Rebelling often, he nevertheless feels secure. He knows where he stands, and— if his early path is delineated for him—where he is going. This applies to both home and school. We have seen what has happened all over the nation where wise school discipline is lacking. And what has come out of homes where discipline, if any, was of the hit and miss variety. Tuesday, shout, threaten, or deprive; Wednesday, forget. . . . The dollar for the movies one day, and the next, the box on the ear.

Life is all discipline. Would we, as parents, take a child to a street corner and turn him loose without cautioning him, telling him what the green and the red lights mean?

If the child does not, early, learn from discipline, he will come to it late, and with anguish.

In addition to the disciplining of those given into our stewardship there is self-discipline, essential in work or play; needed in the conduct of office and household, in every department of human behavior. It can operate in apparently trivial ways, setting up barriers against irritations and pettiness and becoming a strong fortress against the invasion of despair. It will not permit itself, wholly, to be overthrown.

Discipline is a spiritual law, enforced neither by scourge nor lash, judgment nor terror, but by intelligent control. To submit to it, without obsequiousness or resentment, is to be free.

License was never liberty, and freedom under spiritual self-discipline is great security.

Discipline begins in self; for every weakness overcome there is strength, for each self-denial, victory and reward. But it goes beyond self and obeys, in happiness and humility, the Law which is not temporal. In true freedom there is no fear— and a man who, for his soul's sake, chooses physical imprisonment is free.

Release from fear is a wonderful guerdon. It is not expected of us that we shall always rise above anxiety. But fear can be conquered, not through affirmations, mantrams, recitations, or even by praying for release, but by acts, trust, knowledge and recognition of encompassing love. No one can do it for us. We must do it for ourselves. . . .

Someone recently said to me that anything can be achieved by "conversion."

Many things have been, not through mere emotional acceptance—which may last a lifetime, or only a year or a day—but through the steady building up of confidence in self, valid resources, and the quiet growth, within the spirit, of knowledge.

"What is man that Thou art mindful of him?"

Whatever man is, God is—of every individual—mindful. He does not sort men into categories of races, nationalities, color, sects and creeds. He thinks, I believe, of man as simply—man.

"Well, at least," someone said to me the other day, "we are better than the savage." But to be "better" one must first establish the outward equalities. Has another had our advantages, education and the assiduous cultivation of what we call the intellect? Can the savage produce the great artist, scientist, financier? No, not yet. Here he is not "equal." But he, too, is man, created, as all others, through the flesh and possessing an immortal spirit. He is as happy as we, although his happiness differs in origin and expression. Also he loves and hates, he hungers and is thirsty. He fulfills his needs, or finds their satisfaction denied to him. He lives his life and, in the body, dies. And whatever, whomever, he may have worshipped—strange gods, or curious idols—he is man.

I have friends, mother and daughter; the head of the family, who spends much time on ships, brought home, after one voyage, a symbolic stone figure from Easter Island.

It is a primitive image. I regard it, when I go to my friend's, and wonder: What does this mean? How many have worshipped it?

I respect it, for if, as God, this symbol was adored, God was in it.

Anywhere, at any time—now, or centuries hence—when a man's eyes lift, as they have for thousands of years, to the extraordinary layers of dust, air and moisture we call the sky, when they look upon moon and stars, or the brilliance of the sun, his spirit stirs, to admit wonder and mystery, which are other names for God and Creation. He may not know who speaks to him but the word is there; in the beginning the word, the Logos.

In June, wherever I am, I go walking. It may be in London, in the dusk, watching the arch of bridges across the river; or on the Cape where June is gentle as a remembered touch, bright as a jewel; or home where birds say good morning. Wherever it may be, I look at the sky . . . softening into half light or building into thunder, bent like a blue bow holding the arrow of the sun, cool as running water, or warm as an unforgotten hand clasp. It is June. Whatever happens, no matter what headlines scream of threat and disaster, regardless of the temper of the times and the huddle of humanity, no matter what has been before or what is to come, I have lived on earth to see another June, and value it.

June is a moment of roses. It will follow May and precede July, no matter what occurs through man's folly and intemperate impatience.

Do not hurry through June. She is one of the delights upon which you can rely. I love her when she is cold and tearful, and when she is warm and provocative. I forgive her for promising flowers and sometimes forgetting to look after them, once they have blossomed.

Give June your heart.

EIGHT

July

IN JULY OUR HABITS ARE APT TO SPRING TOWARD THE LAZY side of summer. We wish we didn't have to work but could sit under a tall green tree with a tall cool glass. Most of us have habits which we say we would like to lose, but few do more than wish we could stop this or that.

I spent an hour or so recently thinking about my inner bad habits—attitudes of mind, some of which seem to slam shut the doors of the heart. The conclusions I came to were highly unpleasant.

Some bad habits are good ones turned inside out—generosity for instance. Only that which springs purely from the spirit is generous. You give of yourself, your substance, or both without thought.

Criticism can become a reprehensible habit. It isn't quite so bad when you keep it to yourself, but even then it nibbles fringes of your mind. When you share it with others, it's worse. I do not mean that people do not commit deeds, say things, flaunt attitudes which you should not accept with approval. If things are contrary to your honest belief, criticism is justified. But keep it to yourself. (I rarely do and greatly regret it.) Try putting yourself in the other person's place to discover why he behaves as he does. You may not find out, but it is well to have tried. If you are free of whatever you dislike in the other person, at least admit that you have not had his heredity, environment or temptation. I have found to my sorrow that many faults I condemn in others are my own also. They hold up a mirror to me; I look into it and, if I am honest, see myself.

Impulsiveness can be good or bad, but I think that it is more often bad. For one lovely gesture, carelessly made, there are so many unlovely ones that result from judging by appearances or jumping at conclusions.

Well, we can't love everybody, that's certain. The laws of attraction and repulsion remain. I sometimes say that a certain person is not "in my vibration." For all of nature does have vibration, if you wish to call it that.

I am impatient with people often; bored more often still. I trust I do not exhibit these attitudes openly, but I may. I have prayed a great deal in an effort to overcome them. I know of no other way to change reactions toward people to whom one is not drawn. I don't mean those with whom we disagree—reasonable people allow the other fellow his opinion—I mean those to whom we are not attracted, by whose personalities we are to some degree, really repelled.

I get so tired, don't you? There are times when despite

all I have—and I have so much for which to be grateful—
I long to put the burden down. It may be sheer physical
fatigue, or mental, or both. Usually it results from anxiety
or the pressure of going from one crisis to another. More
often than not these are minor, but they do pile up and
the load seems heavy. I know I *can't* lay it down. I know the
fatigue, the despair or panic, will pass, but for that moment
I am a child who finds everything too difficult, looks for a
shoulder to cry on and gentle arms to rock him to sleep.

I don't suppose I ever pray that anyone I love should be
spared the normal vicissitudes of life, for only in facing trouble and responsibility does anyone mature. But there are
times when I do feel that a long, hard path could be smoothed
for them just a little.

For myself I have learned to ask, not that obstacles be
removed, but that I shall be shown the way around them.
Usually I've put the obstacles there myself, so it is up to me
to take them away or bypass them without stumbling.

As I have said, one of the loveliest gifts God ever gave—
and He has given it to us all if we but look for it—is quietude.
I still cannot explain the feeling. I tried to before. It isn't
peace exactly, and it certainly isn't the stupor of complacency,
or sitting with hands folded waiting for manna to fall from
the sky. I cannot explain the feeling of quietude. It is in an
inner stillness, an awareness of being close to the Source of
all life and love. I experience it often, at night or in the early
morning, or when I sit alone and—this is rare—uninterrupted,
looking out a window at the doves upon the grass, or a sunset coloring the clouds.

I wish I could feel this all the time, but I cannot. It rarely reaches me when I am working or playing, certainly not when I am rushing about under pressure of all the usual emotions which come to most people in any given day— worry, fear, brief happiness, pleasant content, meeting people, liking or not liking them, reading, writing, balancing a checkbook, looking at an engagement pad or fretting about a crowded calendar.

The moments rush past and the hours, and it's another day, utterly without quietude, except in the moments of being alone. Even then I have to think and pray myself into it.

I wish that I could reflect quietude always, that it would reach from the inner spirit to the outer man, so that all who came in contact with me would feel it without a word being said. Words are undesirable here, for words would destroy it.

I have known a few people who seemed in their complete undivided personalities to express spirit through the outer physical shell. These were not saints or mystics, or the people whom I have thought over-saccharine. These were normal, busy, happy and useful people. Yet I have known many others who would answer that description, but had not the gift of living with quietude and imparting it.

One who had such a gift was my mother's mother. She lived with us and died, at eighty-five, while I was abroad during the First World War. Grandmother was a semi-invalid for years. Toward the end of the time I knew her she lived, except through her Bible, largely in the past. My father had a Bible specially bound for her in several large, light volumes with big print. She would sit in the big chair in her bedroom and read. And she comprehended, even though, when I came in, she might tell me what she had been "doing," and whatever it was belonged to a remote past, long before I was born.

Yet, always the quietude. When she began to be physically, though not mentally, handicapped, her sense of humor was strong and direct and her wisdom simple and true as the earth. My father took her sailing in his small craft for she was the only woman he knew, he said, who kept her head and also her last meal! I remember her at Cape Cod when I was very small and we had rented a bigger boat for the summer. I have old snapshots of Grandma, wearing a black dress with printed flowers and a large black bonnet, impervious to winds, calms, seasickness and the antics of younger generations.

Grandmother had, in addition to quietude, a gift for silence. It isn't the same thing. One is inward, one is outward. She was moderate in all things, except in believing and loving. Yet in loving her children and grandchildren she was not demonstrative. You just knew she was there with practical and spiritual help. I remember a big kitchen in our first city house and myself skating around in the adjoining, so-called "help's living room." I don't know what I skated on, or with; not roller skates, I am sure. I recall only that my grandmother came downstairs and told me I had better cease and desist. Though normally an obedient child, I didn't stop, and she warned me, "If you don't, you will get your comeuppance."

A little while later I fell and almost knocked out a front

tooth, a second tooth. It dangled by a gruesome thread. I wept. Grandmother called my mother. She flew downstairs and—fortunately it was late spring—dragged me, hatless, bloody and not unbowed, to the dentist, who clapped the tooth back again and told me, in effect, to stay off it for a time. That meant milk, mush and soup.

The tooth's still with me.

Grandmother had warmth, yet a gentle reserve. She accepted everything in her life, I think, small and large, as if she knew that even small things were God's will. We used to laugh at her, lovingly, because when my father served her at the table and asked would she have a second helping, she always responded, "I've a great plenty, thank you."

She was a temperate eater, and once he thought to catch her out by giving her a meagre portion. He could hardly wait for her plate to be cleared—she always cleared it as her mother had taught her to—before asking if she would have more. The answer came serenely, but with a slight twinkle. "I've a great plenty," said Grandmother.

I daresay she always had.

I wish I had known her better. But in my teen stage and later, when she was confined to her room, it was a case of rush in and out and "Hello, Grandma," and "Goodbye, Grandma." I often think of all she could have taught me. Yet looking back, I know she taught me something I did not recognize then. She taught me about quietude, and I am very grateful.

My father was devoted to her. When we were in the country, she was taken to the table in a wheel chair, and to the porch where she would sit like a small queen and hold court. I recall now that she listened more than she spoke, but when she did speak everyone listened.

An old friend, a wonderful nurse, who had been with my mother when I was born, came to ask Grandma's advice. The nurse was past middle years and had worked hard all her life. Now, visiting us in the country, she said that she had been offered marriage by a widower who had two daughters. Should she or should she not accept?

Grandma briefly pointed out the danger of a woman set in her ways marrying a man who was set in his, and the difficulties of mothering grown children. She also remarked that, on the other side of the scales, was companionship—provided they were compatible—and a certain amount of security.

Grandma's conclusion was that, if Harriet and her elderly beau loved each other, if Harriet gave God her problem and followed a sober rather than a fanciful heart, everything would surely be all right.

Perhaps Grandma's advice to one woman is good for every woman in any circumstances: Give your problem to God and follow a sober heart.

I wish I had learned her secret of loving, practical speech, listening silence and wonderful tranquillity.

I knew little of her ancestry, nor asked. I wasn't interested in family trees until too late. When my children began to ask this and that, I rarely knew the answers. (And this doesn't apply to family trees only!) Father's family history was carefully written up by hand in one of those horrible little books with windows in it and names set in. I could never figure how the windows went. Mother's background was a mystery to me except that her father (whom I never knew), was a Quaker from Virginia, with, of all things, North of Ireland blood, way back. He came to New York and married Grandmother. Of Grandmother herself, my knowledge was scant; a farmer's daughter from a village near the city, her maiden name was all I knew. I wondered later: Had Grandfather married out of meeting?

He could have done just that. I knew his father was somewhat whimsical, for he named Grandfather after an obscure English poet. The poet's name was James Hervey, and I had never heard of him. In fact, I didn't believe he had really existed until I ran across a couple of lines ascribed to him in the Oxford book of quotations. The name Hervey, however, went right on: it was my mother's middle name, also my cousin Paul's, and I named my older daughter Hervey. She is completely baffled when my English friends call her Harvey, which is, of course, the way it is pronounced in England and what the original James Hervey must have called himself.

Tonight, while I was writing this, it occurred to me to telephone my cousin, Jessie, and ask her, "Was our grandmother a Quaker?"

She thinks so. She told me that Grandmother's people came originally from Nova Scotia—so I am more confused than ever—and that she and Grandfather attended the Methodist church because, when they lived in Greenwich Village, there was no Friends' Meeting House nearby.

All of this brings me to what I was going to say—until I decided to telephone Jessie—which is that Grandmother's Quaker upbringing probably accounted for a good deal of her silent listening and her personal quietude. She was taught to "center down."

I owned, until I gave it to my older daughter, a Paisley shawl. My mother had it, then I did. She always said it was her mother's wedding shawl. I could never fathom how Grandmother could wrap that great thing about her, put on her bonnet, and sally off to church, for she was not a big woman and the shawl is immense. It is also worn thin in places. At the time it came to me I wrote my Aunt Mary, Jessie's and Paul's mother, mentioning the shawl. It was not long before her death at a few days short of one hundred, but she relayed a message to me. "What," she inquired, I assume in mild disdain, "would a poor farmer's daughter be doing with a Paisley shawl? No," said Aunt Mary, "her husband gave it to her after their marriage and, later, one was given her by a friend." So there were two. Which I had I'll never know until sometime, perhaps, I'll see my grandmother, ask her pardon for my young indifference and neglect, and inquire about shawls.

Funny, how the bits and pieces of family history grow into legends, or fade away. I had always thought Mother's father was born in Harpers Ferry. I drove through it once and wrote Aunt Mary about it. She replied, through her daughter, with considerable calm. "He was born," she said, "in Winchester, Virginia!"

Grandmother used to say that, given time, everything

would work out. I suppose so, but sometimes the time seems overlong. I know that for too many years I have had the sensation of sitting on the edge of a volcano. Just this afternoon, I said that to my friend, Rita, who replied that matters, for most of us, weren't so dramatic. She said, "It's more like always carrying an umbrella. The big storms don't come too often, but you get tired of continuous drizzle and of carrying the umbrella!"

I fancy she's right. I am sure that, among other lessons, there's one to be learned from umbrella carrying.

One of the hardest is that, although you wholeheartedly believe something, you can't always—or altogether—practice it. Grandmother did, I'm sure. But not most of us. For years I have been telling myself that, under Spiritual Law, I am required to love all people and peoples. Sounds so simple; and isn't.

"Love thy neighbor," we are admonished.

It took time to learn that, while I might not even like my neighbor—and I use the word "neighbor" in a general sense—I could, impersonally, love him. It wasn't intended that we love everyone personally. For me, intended or not, it is an impossibility.

Impersonal loving isn't easy, either. We meet all sorts of people; some rub us the wrong way, some bore or anger us. We aren't on the same wave length. Hence, to love them sounds like the solution to an equation, which we can't believe, though we know it's right.

I recall that one spring in the West Indies I met a number of people of varying kinds, hues, colors, religions, races. . . . They could conceivably be sorted into bad, indifferent and good. But, by whom? Not, I think, by me—for who am I to judge who is good or bad or indifferent?

Certainly, God does not expect me to rush about overflowing with sweetness and light, both of which are quite alien to my nature, loving equally those who appear good or bad to me. But He does expect me to recognize that all souls, however obscure to the critical eyes of fellow human beings, are important to Him.

This isn't easy to comprehend, and it is harder to put into practice. Take, for example, the people who bore me. I am bored by what appears to me complete triviality, and quite as bored by deadly seriousness. I am bored by lack of humor as well as by alleged humor of the bubbling-over, practical, or impractical, joker. I am bored by what seems to be stupidity—the crass kind, or the repetitious. I am bored by people who do not share my interests (just as they are bored by me).

There is no remedy except to try to find a meeting ground, a common interest. Even someone quite alien to you, as far as education, background and thinking are concerned, will have some interest which parallels one of yours. It may be flowers or books; it could be bird watching or politics; perhaps it is the theater or the movies; possibly it is cooking or grandchildren. It doesn't matter. There must be something you can mutually understand and, once you have found it, you will get along very well. And if you get along, the impersonal love isn't hard to manage.

After that, you can approach the basic things. This

person whom I don't especially like, with whom I have nothing in common but a passion for oysters or ballet or mystery novels, is flesh and bone and blood; so am I. Stab him and he'll bleed; I will, too. This man has been born as I have been, through a channel of physical suffering; he has in his lifetime known joy, sorrow and fear, and has in his own way worshipped God. Therefore, however different we may appear on the surface one to the other, we are brothers, in human experience, in common mortality and in the immortality of the spirit.

I do not say that this attitude turns one into a saint. For we believe and don't practice. I have admitted these things for years but often come away from a gathering as sharply critical of my fellow guests as I ever was, with this difference—I *know* I have been critical and I am sorry for it. Not that being sorry makes up for censure, but at least I have recognized failure in myself. So, all through our lives, we try, fail and, if we think deeply enough, we try again.

I was a child who went to Sunday school and, when I recited my lesson, I sometimes received at my teacher's hand a gold star. This I pasted on a card. When I had enough gold stars, I was given a book as reward. Usually the book was not of great interest to me, but at least I had, I felt, earned it. I do not expect, now that I am no longer a child in years, that God will give me gold stars, or a reward. But I hope I get "E" for effort.

Not long ago I had occasion to tell a fairy story. It isn't a pleasant one. I read it when I was very young, tried to forget it and thought I had succeeded. But all remains in the subconscious, so some fifty or more years after I first read it, I recalled it. And it kept returning to me, over and over, until I was forced to find some interpretation which would be helpful.

I don't recall its origin. I know only that in its bare bones, so to speak, it is a dreary, frightening little tale.

It concerns a young man deeply in love with a young woman. As a proof of that love she demanded from him the heart of his mother. So he brought it to her, as I recall, upon a platter. On his way he fell three times, and three times the heart of his mother cried out, "My child, did you hurt yourself?"

Once having recalled this grim bit of folklore, I tried to find in it something which, to me, would be completely valid. And this is what I thought:

God's heart pulses through us and the world. Therefore, when we stumble and fall, He speaks, saying not, "My child, you have hurt me," but asking, "My child, have you hurt *yourself?*"

Each failure hurts us. When by error, by falling, we injure ourselves, the Compassion which watches over us is concerned, for our sakes.

Living alone now, it is wonderful to realize that I am not really alone; that there is no time of day or night when I cannot find help; that "underneath are the everlasting arms." I do not expect my personal problems to be solved in an eye's twinkling. I no longer look, as they say, for pie in the sky, as I did when a child. I know that I, myself, must solve my problems and, if there is pie, I have assembled the ingredients and baked it. But I know—as surely as I know I now live, and shall, according to His promise, live forever—that I may ask for guidance in the solution of my little puzzles, for the best possible recipe for the pie before I put the ingredients together.

In all my years I have overcome so little. I have not overcome dreaming, or wishful thinking, or self-seeking, or vanity; neither have I wholly conquered envy, nor cleansed of error my attitude toward others. But I have vanquished fear for myself—if not for those I love. I am not afraid of illness or death in the body, or of accident—whether on a stair, in a plane, a ship, a car or a train. I am now indifferent to what people may think or say of me if I believe that what I have said or done is right. I no longer shrink from being criticized, secretly or openly; from being misunderstood or—which is more crushing—too well understood. I was once afraid of people, as well as of physical heights. I am no longer. I was always afraid of sorrow until I saw it, whole, and face to face.

These are my only, and very incomplete victories, yet I still hope to achieve that "E" for Effort.

I used to be afraid of my own shadow. Now I wouldn't be afraid if I didn't cast any shadow at all!

Someone said to me late last spring, unseasonable with its winds, rains and snowfalls, "Spring will never come." But that fear was, of course, unfounded. Spring always has come. So has summer. And autumn.

It's odd to go in a few hours from climate to climate. I left New York one cold, blowing day, and in six hours

I was wishing I could shed most of my clothes. For about two weeks, while I was looking for shade on a beach or thankfully hailing a taxi on a sun-baked street, my friends up North were going out cautiously in galoshes and fur coats. On the day I returned home I left the hot climate at ten in the morning and around three in the afternoon I was looking out the window of a plane at piles of dirty snow, and at people on the airfield huddled in overcoats and blue with cold.

Don't talk to me about time and space!

Waiting for a doctor to emerge from a sickroom is a matter of eternity, even if he entered it only ten minutes ago. Waiting for your best beau can be forever, though he may be only ten minutes late (or you ten minutes early). Though you may have spent years with people you love, when suddenly you are no longer with them, it seems you have been cheated. Those years couldn't have been more than minutes, you tell yourself, remembering.

Today I had a letter from a friend. I have not met her, yet we have known each other a long time. Her interests lie in charity. I came in touch with her through these interests and we write to each other at intervals. Not long ago she wrote that she had to give up one of her benevolent activities because her doctors had told her that her heart was not strong. I answered that I envied her, and today her letter came, admonishing me for what she must have thought a very negative attitude, and assuring me that I had many years left in which to accomplish things of value, and that therefore I should "want to live."

[141]

How easily a common language is misinterpreted. I hadn't said I didn't want to live. I meant I envied her possibly shorter span.

Years ago, I wrote an article in which I said I had often been despairing but never "suicidal." This was afterwards published, together with others, in a little book. At the time I wrote the article, what I said was true. By the time the book was published, it was not.

I am not proud of that period in my life, but it taught me something. I now understand people who feel the impulse, however curbed, toward self-destruction. I even understand those who cannot curb it. Many are—or were—as I, brought up in the Christian belief. Mine, I thought, sufficed. But when the axe fell and I looked for help, I found none. Not, as I know now, because it wasn't available—help is always there—but because I had shut myself away from it. My belief had not been durable.

When I returned to it, a thousandfold—and with so much help from people who took me, patiently and lovingly, back to my belief and turned it, for me, into knowledge which is more reliable than believing—I thought of the way I had come as a tunnel, long and black. At first, in such a spot, you lie flat on your face; later, you struggle to your knees (which is a good place to start from), and then to your feet. Presently, you begin to walk slowly, and after a while, faster, and then you see light—dim, perhaps; gray certainly; but it increases as you move on. So you know that the tunnel will end and that, outside it, there will be the full blaze of sun.

So I have come to a time, or a way, of thinking which is simple. I am happy when a day ends; and equally so when the next begins. I wish so to live that I need never be afraid to die. I am not afraid, in the ordinary sense, but I would like to go from one room to the next, without apprehension, and with wonder.

I told my correspondent that I "envied" her because I had recently had a routine medical check-up. My doctor discovered, to his amusement, that my heart is seventy per cent horizontal, yet functions within the normal range. I thought it hilarious—for if a horizontal heart is appropriate to anyone, it certainly is to me. I told him that I was sorry my heart was, in its horizontal manner, so well behaved, for it seems to me that of all ways to take one's departure the cardiac way is the easiest. Besides, a cardiac, as a rule, takes good care of himself, is cared for by those about him, and lives, oftener than not, to a ripe old age. At which point my physician remarked that unfortunately one does not usually select one's own exit.

He himself died not long thereafter as the result of a coronary.

That's all I meant when I answered my friend's letter, for I was then, and am now, content to live on earth as long as God so wills. And I shall try to live as fully as possible. That's what I was put here to do.

Every day we live brings wonder if we are aware of wonder, and every night we experience a marvel, which is sleep, not fully explicable even to scientists. Every day we wake is a beginning, but no night an end.

[143]

As I write, I am planning ahead. This is one of the most useful things anyone can do—even if the plans never materialize. At the time I was emerging from my tunnel, I woke one morning with an exact plan for a round-the-world airplane trip in my mind. I knew dates, places, and even how I must order my household while away and how to cope with the clothes necessary for three months in three climates. In making this plan I assumed I had a future, as the trip was to be seven months distant. For quite a while I had been unable to visualize a personal future, any place at all.

So, now I think of various plans: of the books—two to be exact—which, after this one, I want to write; of next spring's projected journey to a part of the world I've never seen; of another Cape Cod summer—the salty dark, the crying gulls, the moving waters, under sun or storm. If before this July ends, I sleep, conscious of dew-wet roses and the sea, and, in the morning, wake to these, warming beneath a rising sun, will it not be a miracle? If, instead, I am here in my own house, or elsewhere in my country, or in another country, or if I am not anywhere visible upon this earth, will it not also be according to a Plan beyond my own and something to look forward to, unquestioning, now?

NINE

August

AUGUST, IN THIS HEMISPHERE, IS A MONTH OF SIGNATURES AND signals. Swallows in the tender dusk perform their skywriting with dark wings; fireflies signal summer, creating transient stars in bush and tree and quiet air. On the beaches the delicate feet of birds autograph the sands; the water, while we sleep, advances and recedes, and in the morning its mark is set upon the shore in driftwood or debris, bits of seaweed and grasses, and shells, tenanted or empty.

In recent years, August has brought hurricane warnings and the dramatic, destructive force of unleashed wind and wave.

One of her frequent signatures is lightning, stabbing with a sharp, bright pen the sky's wide scroll. For a number of years I watched thunderstorms undismayed. Then, when I was in my late teens, riding in a car on a summer evening, the pen stabbed into a nearby tree and my hand, resting on the metal coat rail, received the transmitted shock. After that I was frightened, and I recall a night on which my father took me out to the front porch and said, as the dark sky opened and the lightning wrote its name, "You never see the flash which strikes you."

I thought it scant comfort.

I remember an August weekend in 1920. My parents were in the city; my uncle and his wife and the Navy airman to whom I was engaged, were with me at the farm. My room was on the ground floor and I was there alone. I do not recall that my sister was in the house at the time. I woke, toward morning, to a world of tumultuous thunder and a room alive with brilliance. For as long as I could, I endured it and then, snatching at a robe, fled upstairs to where my uncle and aunt were sleeping—if anyone could sleep.

They woke as I hammered on their door, obligingly let me in, and I crawled into my aunt's bed and immediately felt much safer. And I thought of the young airman in the guest room next door. How concerned he must be for me!

The storm cleared at dawn and I went downstairs again. No sound had come from the guest room. No appearance until breakfast, at which I inquired of my fiancé, with some annoyance, how he had fared during the storm.

"What storm?"

I could have flung the coffeepot at him. Insensible creature, not only endowed with the ability to relax completely when he was not on duty, but wholly unaware of the pathetic timidity of the young woman who was (presumably) the apple of his eye!

My uncle and aunt—he was only thirteen years or so my senior, and I called him and his wife by their given names —laughed heartlessly.

In later years, when I had children of my own, I was determined to rule out as many fears as I could. In the Brooklyn house, near the Narrows, I instructed the two good, loyal girls who helped me that no matter how frightened they were of storms they were, in no circumstances, to display fear before the children.

Poor things, they were terrified, but they obeyed. When thunder crashed and lightning exploded, they kept their promise, although I often saw them turn dusky lavender under their dark skins. While all three of us clenched our teeth against chattering, the children rushed to windows, considering the spectacle entirely for their benefit. When they were older and spent their summers with close friends on the St. Lawrence, they witnessed violent storms, and across the water, saw barns struck into torches. I used to be with them for a month and was delighted at the effect the household calm had had upon them. By that time they knew it was neither wise, nor permitted, to be in a boat or romping in the water like dolphins during a storm. But none was afraid, and my younger daughter, taking due precautions, was apt, during the worst storms, to put on rubber boots and a raincoat and go off to the houseboat pulled up on the narrow beach to watch the celestial fireworks from its deck.

As time went on and they learned what can happen, and often does, they lost this innocence. I am certain that the

girls are not happy in thunderstorms now, although they
will drive their cars through the worst of them. One claims
it is the noise that bothers her, not the lightning. I don't
know. I had done my best to remain a papier-mâché rock
of strength and completely hypocritical serenity.

Now, I don't have to pretend because all my children
are grown and accustomed to Mamma's vagaries. I could
clutch at the arm of one of the six footers and howl like a
dog, and he would pat me on the head and say "There, there."
The girls, too, would rally to the maternal emergency.

But it so happens that I'm not frightened any more.

I don't like storms. I don't like to see or hear them.
When they occur at night, I pull down blinds and shades
and unplug radios and the television set. My telephone is
right beside my bed. The line leading to it often receives
a glancing blow and the bell tinkles happily. Aware of this
I put the telephone on the floor as far from the bed as
possible. There's a flashlight beside me, too, because sometimes the lights flicker and—if a branch falls and strikes
a wire—go out. The electricity often goes on again before
I can decide: Shall I or shall I not call the company and see
how long this will take? It doesn't matter in summer, unless
the power is off long enough to defrost freezer and refrigerator.
Besides, I have a generator, and can use it, if repairs take any
length of time, always provided I have the courage to go
down two flights of stairs to the cellar with the flashlight.

This is a frame house, and has stood for many years.
Right outside the east windows of the living room, and
growing up past the sun porch on the second floor, there

is an ancient mulberry tree, three quarters gone as a result
of blizzards, hurricanes, ice storms and age, but still mam-
moth and heavily leafed. I once said to someone, "If the
mulberry tree ever falls, it will take the sun porch and come
right into my bedroom," and he replied carelessly, "Oh, they
always fall the *other* way!"

This is consoling, but I'd like to know how he knew.

The night appears longer during a storm; by day they
never seem as protracted. I used to be restless, tense and
even develop a headache before one struck; something in
the atmosphere communicated the warning to me. That has
passed, for this house is equipped with lightning rods, caus-
ing the electricity to descend, so I'm told, into the ground.
And I am no longer nervous. I dread fire, having experienced
one; I despise any loud noise, and I don't like the way
lightning looks, although I admit it has a singular beauty,
but, for myself, I feel no apprehension, even when I am
alone, which is most of the time.

Hurricanes I have lived through without fear. I do
not know why. The first one which neared me was in Puerto
Rico. My husband and I, having packed a few belongings,
waited for a car which would take us from the sugar planta-
tion into the nearest town before matters became too difficult. I was as absorbed as if I were watching a drama—as
indeed I was. I remember, at this great distance, the color
of the sky before the storm, a strange sullen yellow. The
little house on stilts shook and the palm trees bent; great
fronds were torn away and crashed to the ground. At the
center of the storm there was the curious peace, the eye,

the complete stillness. That hurricane lashed us only with the winds about its fringes, veered away, and we presently went back into the house and unpacked.

In recent years we have had hurricanes on this coast. I've seen them at home and on Cape Cod. It is a strange thing—I do not like ordinary wind, strong and gusty, especially in winter, nor the eerie sounds it makes in the chimneys —yet in the untamed wind of hurricanes, and the tons of falling, blowing rain, I have struggled out to a car or walked, bent double, down the hill to pool my emergency resources with my friends, Gladys and Eleanor.

Nor do winter storms do much more than inconvenience me. Last February we had a wild, white storm. It began on a Saturday night, just as friends arrived to drive me to their house for dinner. We had been warned by the weather bureau, and to the north of us people had been digging themselves out of over three feet of snow, and lives had been lost.

But when I went out to the car, the snow was thin, meagre and rather listless, not falling in big white flakes which had introduced the blizzards I remembered. Returning home, before eleven, we crept through a blinding whiteness.

By Sunday morning, the wind blew from every direction; the ploughs were on the highways, but not effecting much; our country roads and my driveway were unploughed, for it simply kept on snowing. Two of the young men who keep an eye on me managed to get to the house and shovel paths which were, not long thereafter, as if no shovel had ever touched them.

[150]

I watched the birds at the feeders; they had some shelter, behind glass, but not much; and plenty of seed when the wind blew the snow away from it. I thought of the precarious lives they lead; we never think of that, except in winter, I imagine. I put out bread crumbs, hoping they would find and eat them quickly before the snow obliterated them. The bird bath had been frozen solid for days and no fluid water was available.

I was comfortable in the house, which was warm, and there was work to be accomplished. For the first time in years the weather prevented me from getting to my church, which is in another town—for I would certainly serve no purpose in risking, not only my mortal life, but that of a taxi driver. For the first time, also, I was not going, after church, to dinner with friends.

As cooking the simplest thing involves more concentration on my part than goes into the solving of mathematical problems, and more steps to and from cupboard, range and sink than a cross-country walker takes on a long trek—between work, the papers, and my nervous preparation of a solitary supper, my day was planned for me.

You are probably thinking that to jump backwards from August to February requires more agility (and makes less sense) than Mark Twain's frog. But what I am really thinking about in August is as valid in February and, indeed, in any month.

I am thinking about storms, all kinds, hatched by nature or ourselves, and remembering everything from blizzards to dust storms, hurricanes, gales and tornadoes, floods and ice, sleet and thunder. No climate seems to pursue a predictable course. I have watched it hail down a Midwestern chimney in May, and in the Arizona desert in March. The first time I went to Palm Springs, in California, more than the entire annual rainfall had descended in a day or two just prior to my arrival. The roads were washed out.

Even when storms come at the proper seasons they can outrun, or laugh at, predictions. I recall an unheralded blizzard, which began late Christmas night, and was followed by an ice storm of unforeseen proportions. I woke to hear the branches of trees falling with reports like gun shots. When the morning sun shone, I realized I had never seen such beauty or a more dangerous brilliance. Every branch, twig and wire was burdened with the hard, thick glitter, and where the sun did not seek out a bush, it appeared gray and unsubstantial-seeming as a cloud of smoke.

That was the time when two members of the household were ill, and the power had failed—it stayed off for days, and weeks—and, as five fireplaces couldn't keep us warm, and the storage supply of water wouldn't last, we decided to go to the city. It took two men to get us to the station, a matter of a few miles. We crept, for what seemed like hours, over glare ice, stopping every few yards so that they could get out and clear tree limbs from the road. At that time, advance hotel reservations were not as necessary as now. When we reached the station, I telephoned New York. The car and the men went away, and we waited for whatever train would next arrive, reached the city, and the hotel, put the invalids to bed, and sent for a doctor.

All storms pass.

The storms which assail us emotionally, disrupting and disturbing our personal lives, pass also, though there are some which leave scars, erosion or total loss. There are high, sudden winds of panic or anger; periods of noise and confusion, made worse by the fear that, at any moment, the irrevocable blow will fall, the lightning strike and stun. There exist in the emotions such drastic changes of temperature as you will not find on a thermometer. . . . There are far-below-zero periods when you seem incased in the bitter cold of unrelenting ice, so frozen you think you will never be warm again. And there are times when the temperature shoots up toward the point of violent explosion.

There are storms, too, like tidal waves. . . . I have seen a tidal wave and years before that the unrepaired devastation one had effected. . . . A tidal wave is an advancing, engulfing, ruthless monster, and those we experience emotionally rise suddenly from the profoundest depths of human despair to tower above the hapless who know not how to escape or whence to flee.

Earthquakes of the natural variety are not unknown to me, although I have never been in a big one, but once I lived in a place where little tremors were so constant that I was never able to keep a picture straight on the walls. Even those afflict you with a sense of utter helplessness.

Many of our personal storms arise without warning: the sky seems cloudless, and suddenly disaster is upon us. Some are so long in the brewing that, looking back, we cannot accurately tell where, when or in what they had

[153]

their origins. Others are swift to come and go—the summer storms, released in tears and followed by the return to sunlight. Some last a moment; some we think will endure forever.

None does; not in nature, and not in the emotional climate of the comparatively normal person who has learned, or is learning, to adjust.

The tree which bends often outlasts the one which stands its ground and yields no inch. In all living, a certain amount of giving before the wind is necessary, a pliancy which is perhaps better called acceptance. In meeting our own personal storms—no matter what proportion they may reach, or how serious they become, predicted or unpredicted —we can learn something from the hurricane. The eye of the hurricane, the meteorologists tell us, is a still, undisturbed flow of air, above which the sky is blue; along which, as in a lane of safety, birds may fly.

In the eye of every storm is God . . . to find Him in prayer, in trust, and in courage, is immeasurable security, for it is to know, understand and accept His will.

He is in all nature: in the storms above and about us, in the storms within us; nothing is barren of Him. When personal catastrophe is upon us, He is there and, as we discover this, the lightning, however it may stun, does not destroy; the crest of the wave does not utterly engulf us; the ice melts, snow ceases to fall, wind and rain and waters abate.

Anxiety is difficult to overcome; fear is a heavy burden; and panic, intolerable. It has never served a useful purpose.

It is panic which traps a man in a burning house, under a tottering ceiling or beneath the tree which is about to fall. Panic erases everything we have ever learned: we forget how to follow instructions, how to swim, where to find shelter, even how to breathe properly.

That is physical panic. There is also the emotional and in that, too, the very tissues of the mind seem torn, the pattern of everything ever known is rent asunder and there is no hiding place anywhere.

In all disasters, the thing most dreaded by those who come to help is panic, for many people who have become as animals create such confusion that further disaster befalls.

I saw on a screen not long ago, a picture of panic. . . . It was certainly a very good performance, acted in the setting where such a thing had actually occurred under the bombings of the last war, and by the people, racially, who had suffered it. Even knowing it was not real, you knew it *had* been, and I, for one, could not for long sit watching.

Three times, as an earlier war shaped itself while I was in Germany, I witnessed mob hysteria: once in a restaurant when people leaped upon tables, shouted, screamed and sang; again when, walking down a broad street, people, without warning, began to run toward one of the embassies, which to them represented an enemy. They had stones in their hands. I did not know why, or where, they were running, but I found myself running with them; and it was not until we reached the embassy building that I realized what was happening. My country was not then at war; I had no enemies. Yet I was affected, and mindless, as if I were blood sister to the unknown woman screaming beside me.

Later, on a night in August, Tante, her daughter and I went with the Commissioner of Police to the station from which the first troops from our section were to depart. It was a hot, still night. The grapevine had been in operation for hours, so the station was crowded with people, milling this way and that, some singing, some shouting and many women weeping. A number were in deepest mourning, although as yet no shot had been fired at their men. As we went through the station with a police guard, someone shouted that we were spies, and suddenly they all seemed at our heels. The policeman pushed them back, shouted with, and at them, and presently we left the building by some further door and were out in the air walking up an incline. There was a siding and upon it the train waited. No one was on the long narrow platform but ourselves, the King of Saxony, his aides and a general in command.

Young men leaned from the windows of the cars, smoked and spoke quietly among themselves. The King walked up and down and spoke to them. He was a big man, and handsome, if my memory serves me. And I recall clearly that the tears ran, unchecked, down his face.

It was quiet there, in the hot night, yet in the background I could hear as one hears in the audience at a play the sound of voices dimmed by distance, rising and falling and coalescing into a sullen murmur. The voices of many people, the mob, hysterical and threatening, laden with foreseen misery. I have never forgotten it.

Those three experiences were engendered by many things, but mainly by panic.

The panic which inwardly assails us may outwardly express itself in any number of ways, but sometimes it does not express itself at all. I have known people who walked among others in total terror, as little aware of the road, as ignorant of where to turn, as blind men in an alien, uninhabited country. Only those to whom their situations were known, guessed. That demands a special kind of courage, and while it is sometimes rooted in pride it is more often born of consideration for others.

Do not for a moment imagine that I write only from imagination or observation. I am no stranger to these evils . . . storms, anxiety, fear, panic. How I behaved outwardly during these times I do not know, and I have never asked anyone who was close to me at such times. In retrospect I can remember trivialities—weather, clothes, gatherings of people and surroundings—but I do not now seem to be the person who walked in the rain or under the sunshine, put on a dress, talked with people, or looked on familiar or unfamiliar places. I was that person; I no longer am—except that what she was is part of what I have become.

There will be no storm tonight unless the wind changes or something I do not understand disturbs the weather pattern. This is a warm night, and lovely; there are many stars. It is a still night.

In our language there are many words which seem to me, born to it as I was, wholly to express their meaning.

Dusk is one, *twilight* another. And the words which express the essence of quietude—as does *quietude* itself: *stillness, silence, tranquillity, serenity, peace* and *calm*. One can set them like jewels on a necklace and wear them for comfort.

All over this land and others it is past midsummer, and the year runs on burning feet toward autumn. Beaches are crowded, mountains are being climbed; boats put out from harbors, picnics are everywhere, and the highways are bumper to bumper with cars. Children on holiday refuse to believe that school will ever open, and older children that, somewhere, there is an office, a factory, a desk or kitchen. The fortunate who can remain, season-long, at the vacation place of their choosing are in less of a hurry to see everything, do everything in two weeks' time.

There will be storms, in summer; there always are. There is no season wholly free of them. And personal skies can darken on a holiday as well as during the routine of home.

No one can ever take a complete holiday from self, his many involved situations; none cuts himself loose from those he loves and their uncertainties. But when a holiday is unmarred by problems, how re-creative. . . . I am not now thinking of those who work so hard at vacationing that they return home more tired than they departed from it, if with another kind of fatigue.

Once you have learned the rudiments, you can go on holidays without moving from your room, and such journeys are as close to a vacation from self as anything can be. I usually take mine in the early morning or during the night. Sometimes, on a day when I am alone, I stop what I am doing and go into another room, idly look at a book, and then, putting it aside, try for a little while to drift.

Some people are endowed all their lives with the ability to dismiss, at will, the questions and problems which nag at them; they can brush them aside as you do a persistent insect, and, addressing them with the proper amount of firmness, say, "Go away."

I once talked to my doctor about this and he recommended that I so speak. He said, "Just say, 'I won't think about you now; come back at three o'clock.'" He then added, "But you must be sure to keep your appointment."

I laughed, for he was so serious, and I thought of Scarlett O'Hara, who always said, "I'll worry about that tomorrow."

Most of us have to go through a long period of self-discipline before we can dismiss what troubles us, ease ourselves into the tide and drift without struggling to turn this way or that. But if you become at all adept, you even learn to conquer your annoyance at interruptions which pull you back to shore again: the telephone bell, the knock on the door . . . friend, stranger, suppliant, or the young voices shouting from the foot of the stairs, "Hi, Mom!"

So the spell is broken before you are deeply enchanted by it, and the glass of the moment breaks all about you. But even if you had three seconds, you are somewhat restored.

Quietude in this August night, stillness, and the hushed stars a lovely sight. Actually, there is sound: a leaf stirs, or a bird; people walk by on the road, a car goes past, a clock strikes, an animal rustles through the grasses. But I hear them only faintly. . . . I went out a moment ago to stand on the stone steps and looked up at the immensity above me. I have said the stars were hushed, yet who knows in what unearthly sound they, too, express themselves, blazing cool in darkness? I cannot identify the animal, now silent, or the bird; the people have passed, the car has gone its way.

No storm tonight.

So I return to the desk, and it's bedtime, and I am wishing for us all a happy summer month, with all storms swiftly clearing, and just enough fireworks to spark our skies.

★ TEN

September

IN THIS SMALL SLICE OF THE ROUND WORLD SEPTEMBER IS A fine month, but it can be hot. I remember one September which seemed to me—because of the heat of the weeks preceding it, and my own emotional disturbance—absolutely unendurable. But generally it's a lovely season.

On Cape Cod, September is wonderfully colored, and the wind is cool at dawn and dusk; the days, usually warm. Swimming is not too cold for my hardier friends, or the sun too hot, or the temperature too low except upon the allegedly "unusual" days, which are deplored by the year 'rounder everywhere. . . . I have been fated to arrive in many places and bring unusual weather with me.

On the Cape the fishing is good and we look for the delectable winter flounder. Scallops are in season, and adventurous striper-fishermen take heart, cast from the golden sands, wade into the waves, and hope. Some linger until

after dark and there are beach fires for them and late pic-
nickers. But the striper, swimming in his native element,
hopes also and, from my experience as an onlooker, is the
more successful.

The trees will begin to turn, suddenly, slightly; the
cranberry bogs will flush with their dark, indescribable color;
the beach plums have ripened. Yet, September seems but
a half hour distant from last May and next. Time is like
a frock, once too long for the child for whom it was personally
fashioned, then just about right for a while, and finally far
too short.

I planned for last summer; I was to go to the Cape
cottage for three months. I had work to do, an unjelled
book, just a few pages, to rewrite, and finish. I didn't do
it. Instead, from the first day of June, I went to so many
places, by car and by plane—crossing an ocean, traversing
a good portion of this country—that I felt like a demented
trainman leaping to the platform to call the names of
distant stations before the train has slowed down to halt
at the first.

I didn't return to the cottage until early August and
came home soon after mid-September in time for the christening of the latest grandchild, in this house, and to get
ready for a visit to a friend and some public speaking in
Alabama.

About this time someone, in all kindness, wrote me
that he thought, at my age, it was time I slowed up—or
did he say down?

Up, or down, it doesn't appear to be in my nature,

at any age, and he should be encouraged by the fact that no matter how far I travel, or how long remain away, I always return thankfully to my own roof and walls, to the sense of belonging and quiet. I have no desire to spend the rest of my mortal life—even if I could—dreaming by a fire, nor, in season, under an apple tree. Not if a million untaxable dollars fell into my astonished hands tomorrow would I erect an ivory tower. I have no use for ivory towers, isolation, or shutting myself away from the flowing stream of living.

There is work to do; there are places to see; some to be revisited in affection and the wish more completely to explore them. Hawaii for instance; London; the Cape. There are people to meet, known and unknown. . . . With old friends it is easy to pick up the threads and weave them into one's pattern again, patching the places which may have worn thin in absence. With new, there are different patterns. All this is stimulating, the familiar horizons widened, the unfamiliar seen.

I have a friend in Maui, Hawaii, whom I have visited several times; she has many interests—her husband, her children, grandchildren and house—and also has effectively run both large houses and small. She occupies herself with civic duties, and is as hospitable as the door which opens on firelight and nourishment. She possesses, fortunately, more vitality than a dozen women, though she has had her share of sorrow, physical difficulties and anxiety.

Frances has a disconcerting habit. When I return with her from an engagement and consider that, for a little time,

I will rest and go slowly from one window to another, to look here at the mountains, there at the sea, she promptly appears in the guest room, happily saying, "Get on your horse. We are going somewhere else."

The horse is figurative, thank heaven, so I get on it.

Hers is an awareness of the stream of life; she wishes swiftly to be carried along it, companioned and useful. If she sometimes overcrowds her hours, that is her nature.

We all know and admire people like her.

Life in this world is certainly a journey, whether or not you ever go beyond your village, town, state or country limits. No matter how far or fast you travel, physically, or in imagination, one day you'll reach home. Half the pleasure in travelling physically is the knowledge that you will return.

To me, as to many, home is a place with a name—a house and the welcome of my family and friends. I have missed them. Have they missed me?

The house is not alive in the usual sense, although any scientist would tell us it is, being a mass of atoms attracted together. But over a period of years, it has come alive to me in an emotional sense, and, while my family and I occasionally clash, I don't clash with my house, don't argue with it. Sometimes I am exasperated when ceilings "done over" a year ago show cracks and the new wallpaper or paint is spotted, or I have to have slipcovers again—but that is not the fault of the house. After 157 years or more it has a right to settle down, every now and then stretch its walls and yawn. As for furnishings, what happens to them is of no concern to the house. All this house asks is peace, warmth when it's cold outside and a cool breeze when it isn't, reasonable care and unreasonable appreciation.

Most houses, like dogs, acquire personality traits of their owners. Not mine. It's independent. It shrugged its shoulders when, in course of time, it found on its roof a chimney which led nowhere. It endured fifty or sixty years of blue paint upon its beautiful pine floors, and also the tedious removal of what must have seemed like several layers of skin. It didn't mind its inside beams being concealed and then exposed, or, I suppose, the painter who last year carefully painted over one of them. (I minded.)

Many people have lived here, old and young. Children were born in this house and have died here, I suppose. The house doesn't care. It doesn't make the least effort to tie an owner to its doorstep. I have a feeling that, when I go away, it may miss me and slumber a little, remembering other years; waking when I come back, opening one shuttered eye and saying, "Well, it's about time."

But it does not have my characteristics. I suppose it really could not take on all the traits of those who have run up the front stairs or walked through the rooms. So it has become itself, quiet except for creaks and rattles during storms, withstanding as it has always withstood, watching trees being planted and growing tall. It may sometimes say, "Seems only yesterday that little tree was no higher than a hoptoad, and now it's past the second-story window!"

When I am cross, the house is not. When I think life is a nuisance to be endured rather than enjoyed, the house pays no attention; when I am excited or gay, apprehensive or uncertain, the house exhibits no such variations in mood. "If she can't keep me," it seems philosophically to say, "someone else will. . . . If she departs for any reason someone else will come."

In this house I like being physically alone for a time in each twenty-four hours; it is restoration. There is no need to respond to anything outside myself. I have almost learned, in part, to dismiss the day from my mind, after quite automatically reviewing it. I am beginning to learn to take no thought for the morrow; at least, for myself.

When, in the spring of 1957, I was on the television program called "Person to Person," it originated here. I was living, as I normally do, alone, which was possibly what interested Mr. Murrow. But I cannot say that the preparation was conducted singlehanded by me; men swarmed outside and in, doing intricate things, for some time prior; and on the day I was televised "alone," there were twenty-five of them in the house.

Person to person, when you think about it, has more meaning than is seen on the surface. First, the television program, when a million or so people are watching other people—person to person. Or the telephone phrase, for instance, meaning to pick up a transmitter and ask, as I did recently, to speak to a stranger in Montego Bay, Jamaica —person to person.

There is one person-to-person call which can be made at any hour, from anywhere—from you to God.

Mornings, drinking tea in bed or coffee by the picture

window; nights, lying against blue pillows with the blue lamp burning, I put in my call, without intermediaries. When I pray, it is aloud; there is none to hear me save God, and what I say is not in any prayer book; it is between Him and me, and He always hears.

Recently, a friend gave me a tiny, round fossil, faintly gray and pink. It is literally millions of years old. I have another which my daughter Ann sent me—a shell incased in a polished, clear jewel, preserving its convoluted shape. Showing these to friends the other night, I thought: Here, in the palm of my hand, I hold the ages, the countless centuries, symbolic of the earth, patiently shaped by time and water, floods and earthquakes. And I thought of beaches I have walked upon—brown or white, black or rosy, composed of the grains of sand which once were rocks and shells, ground, over the years and years, by the sea and the tides, into playgrounds for children, who build castles and watch them wash away.

It makes you ponder on the relative brevity of human life—and that of the bird, animal, fish and reptile, which, except in a few instances, is so much shorter. We, too, are shaped by disasters and upheavals in a small space of time. And it appears part of human nature to be aware of the terrible, stubborn inability to be still and know.

As a child, I hoped that someday school would end and lessons be over; I know now school is eternal and lessons also.

Each of us mourns over things we longed and prayed

for, which never were granted . . . the luminous, impossible dreams, the fulfillment of which was not given. But the most profound grief is for that which once we possessed and which has—we think—been taken from us. For, as Tennyson said, "a sorrow's crown of sorrow is remembering happier things."

I once saw another version—"happiness remembered, which is no more."

One of the compensations of growing old is that you can, with whatever difficulty, grow into acceptance of the withholding, the taking and sorrow's crown. That is when you begin to learn to be still and know; to give over, and let go.

Yet sorrow's crown need not be. Nothing valid and real is ever lost, and remembered happiness can still be just that. It is not visible to the outer sight, it cannot be heard by the physical ear, or touched with the hands. All that has existed in truth still exists, it has not even been mislaid. It is the *way* we regard remembered joy that can make it sorrow's crown; if we see it with resentment and despair, it reaches us as darkness; if, with gratitude and acceptance, as light.

There are many times when I cannot visualize the faces of people I love, who appear to have left me for a time. I do not have the type of memory which reproduces features wholly and accurately; and all photographs, however good the likeness, lack much, for the sitter is caught in one static moment. But I am fortunate in that I can see, in flashes, an expression, a characteristic gesture. There was a time when I refused to make the attempt; later, I tried, and sometimes succeeded; now I do not try at all. When someone comes into my mind who is wholly and indelibly in my heart, I visually remember, without effort, for a moment. It is always a transitory glimpse, but a true one.

A woman, writing me that she could not achieve inner quiet, said that she thought people were born with, and could not acquire, it. She is preoccupied with serious problems and her physical health, and is essentially lonely. She is right as far as she goes. People are born with it—all people; for like the joy of which I earlier wrote, it is a quality of the spirit. Many do not seem, as she says, to "acquire" it, because they give it neither credence nor recognition. They are so overlaid with wrappings of anxiety, fear, unhappiness—oh, a hundred things . . . like the White Queen's shawls—that they cannot reach past these, within, to the center of quiet, nor can it outwardly manifest.

She asked, "How is it possible to go aside and be still?"

It is certain that men, under the pressure of earning their livings, and returning home to families, obligations and problems; and women, conducting households and fulfilling varied duties; and even those without families, who return to their places of residence, late and tired, find it difficult to set aside a definite time for withdrawal. Those who are praying people seek it in prayer, by day and night. But the deliberately quiet time which acts as recreation and restorative is hard to achieve. Yet, during any given day, at least a few minutes can be taken from the busiest working and playing life.

For God, Who is all-quiet, is everywhere present. He is in kitchen and study, corridor and office. He is in the playroom and on the stairs. No room is closed to Him, no reaches of the land unknown. He is in factory and restaurant, in school and railway station, as He is in church and mosque and temple. He is on highways and country roads, on lonely or crowded streets, on plane and ship and train. Wherever we are, there He is, for there is no place without Him, and He is our refuge and our strength.

All space, which is God, is never empty. We conceive of it in various ways, the scientist differently than the untutored. We think with amazement and scant under-standing of man-made satellites, revolving in their orbits, and consider the possibility of future journeys into vast obscurities. But all this we devise in our conscious minds.

True space is within us, a dimension of the spirit. Look within for space, God-filled. We ourselves, however insignificant, however transitory upon earth, move in limit-less space and in many dimensions. We do not function only through that which can be seen and touched. We reach into dimensions of love and knowledge, move in those of spiritual understanding—apart from, yet part of, our mental, emotional and physical expressions. We are nowhere bound but wholly free, for we occupy in spiritual consciousness a spatial universe unrestricted and immeasurable.

The consciousness of the physical mind reaches bound-aries and retreats, but the eternal consciousness of the spirit knows no limitations. Once this truth becomes apparent, however dimly, we are loosed, released from time and outward, even unseen, space. Then, we need not go apart in order to discover confidence and quiet. It is good to do so, for the relaxation which follows is reflected in our physical and mental states. But if we are unable to find one moment in the waking hours to dedicate to peace, we can yet withdraw to the center, not only of our own beings, but of the universe. We may be talking or working, at a desk or on an assembly line, we may be anywhere, but there is always the opportunity.

Under all preoccupations, there is the waiting stillness, like the voiceless center of the hurricane.

Psychiatrists often tell patients they cannot do two things at once. But two things we can truly do: lead, simultaneously, the inner and the outer lives.

Even outwardly two things can be done at once by the normal person. Haven't you answered a telephone sensibly while taking accurate notes, or heard a conversation and made comments while writing a letter? Haven't you listened to the radio while working or studying? Perhaps, in such instances, the doctors would say, "But you couldn't do either thing well!"

As a young girl in the First World War, living in Germany with the older friend whom I have mentioned, she would read aloud, evenings, to me and to her daughter. We were both supposed to improve our minds; I was required to better my German. As Tante read, she knitted with incredible accuracy and speed. She never looked at the knitting, only at the book. She would free a hand to turn a page or a sock, but missed no word and dropped no stitch.

During this period I was taught to knit, as Tante did not approve of idle hands. Her daughter embroidered beautifully. I was set to fashioning scarves, as these presented fewer difficulties to the beginner, casting on, and casting off, than other articles. I remember only one scarf. Lumpy and strange, it grew like the beanstalk and seemed without end. I was reminded of my clumsiness and unusual concentration, when, a while ago, I saw a motion picture in which Alec Guinness played a brilliant, if lunatic, plotter. He always wore a long knitted scarf which, at intervals, he flung dramatically over his shoulder, or wound more closely about his neck. As Mr. Guinness moved close to his just deserts, the scarf practically dragged upon the ground. And so I thought of my handiwork. I doubt that it ever reached its presumed destination. Tante was far too tender-hearted—and practical—to impose an alien, deadly weapon upon any member of any army. That scarf would have meant certain strangulation.

I have never knitted since. I know myself, not only as a step-retracer, but as an incurable stitch-dropper. You don't have to purl one and count two, or whatever it is, to drop stitches, create uneasy protrusions, inexplicable holes, or ruin a pattern.

Figuratively speaking, we all begin to knit when young. I don't know how your knitting has turned out, but mine is what one of my dearest friends would have called a mish-mash. When spread before me—the work of almost sixty-two years, if you presume I began to knit at three —I am horrified. There are, I am happy to say, a few rows which are quite well executed, and patterns which have glowing color, and even some beauty . . . but oh, the gaps, the humps and dropped stitches!

Here I have dropped a stitch of loyalty and there of truth; further along are the patched-up places where the row went in the wrong direction and I later tried to bring it into order. Here are all the mistakes caused by unevenness of emotion, wrong decisions; and the gaps of remorse and regret, which patching didn't help. The big sins and little were cast on and, where I tried to cast them off, there is confusion.

In many places the pattern is almost lost in a welter of wrong stitches. Where for a short space it emerges clearly as it should be, I am humbly grateful. People say that when they reach what are sometimes thought of as the Gates of Heaven, they will present a sober list of assets and liabilities to the Gatekeeper. I shall have nothing to offer but what I have made of the original fabric of my life. In short, my knitting. And I shall ask the Gatekeeper: How am I to remedy it?

I believe that there is much I shall have to unravel and re-knit, righting, as best I can, the mistakes.

I seem to have strayed a long way from September but then the months dissolve one into the other, and this month is no more and no less important than the last. We mark months on a calendar or by the change in situation, and season. Now the trees feel the first warmth of the match which will set them flaming before this month has run. Down under, in Australia and New Zealand, people look hopefully toward sky and tree and assure themselves it's spring.

Our birds have not left yet, and some will remain throughout autumn and winter if there is shelter and food; and that there will always be, whether I am here or not, as long as these acres are in my possession. The migrants, those which stay a day or two or even only minutes, have not yet appeared—but those which have been with us summer long are starting to flock, and consult their leaders before they take off for parts unknown to me.

In September, I look at my anniversary book, as I do every month. This month marks the twelfth wedding anniversary of my son, Hugh, and his wife, Janet, and the first anniversary of the christening of their baby girl. It is the anniversary of my parents' marriage, and all through the month there are the birthdays of friends. Mine is next month. Shall I look ahead to it with apprehension, and regret? Shall I wish myself back a dozen, two or three dozen years?

No!

I like it the way it is. I would not go back in sidereal time for anything this world could promise me . . . not for youth, or for beginning again. For youth is with each of us always, if we live to be a hundred, and it is impossible to begin all over again. I cannot unravel the knitting now and start with the virgin wool, the shining empty needles.

I am content when the September moon rises, a sliver or a sphere; when the evening star burns low upon the horizon and the sky is ineffably colored. Over any water, sunsets are particularly spectacular, because of the reflection. I have watched sunsets on the Atlantic and the Pacific, over the Thames in New England and the Thames, arched with bridges, in old England. I have seen it mauve and golden, reflected in a pond in Molokai, Hawaii, as Japanese fishermen moved through the waters with their nets. During one weekend I saw sunset broken into stained-glass fragments in the swift-running waters of a New Zealand river. Long ago, from my father's house, I watched the miracle on water which came winding down a creek into a quiet place. When we lived in Brooklyn, we were near the Narrows; and, for many summers, I saw the sunset on the St. Lawrence River, so beautiful my heart ached, and I could have eaten the colors with a spoon.

In recent years I have been witnessing sunsets here . . . those in winter bring a special blessing . . . and I watch them on Cape Cod.

In September, as in other months, Gladys Taber takes me out after supper. We drive to the post office and note, after Labor Day, how tranquil the village, the tumult and the shouting of the busy season having died. Sometimes we go to look from heights upon beaches which fringe the ocean, at the Coast Guard Station on Nauset Light. These do not face the west, but there is always a luminous sky and moving waters, calm or disturbed. Sometimes we go to the wharf at Rock Harbor and watch the fishing boats come home in the last illumination. More often, we drive across the narrow land to Skaket, which sounds harsh, and isn't; or to First Encounter, which sounds exciting, and is, the Pilgrims having, on this beach, first encountered its owners—the Indians.

Skaket Beach has a special magic; here particularly the sunset is a living glory; and, you contemplate a forever-anchored ship, a distance out, dark against sky and water. Color is constant in the sky; even dusk, when it comes, is tinted. Light lingers and, if the tide is low, the sands are exposed for a long way, and there are charcoal pools washed with rose and umber. Children run with dogs upon the dry portion of the beach, or wade in the pools and among grasses. Gulls create dark designs. Always, there are parked cars here and people in them to watch the shifting hues of sand, water and sky, and look for the boats which silently return.

When I was young, many Septembers since, I had an integral appreciation of beauty, careless and easy. Often, I tried to put it into rhymed words, usually bad, at best mediocre. Now, I merely look, as if this sunset were the last I'd ever see. I can feel each, warm in the marrow of my bones and in my blood. I take it into myself as nourishment, and taste it with the consciously delighted palate of the mind, the slow, mute savoring of the spirit.

All sunsets anywhere, anytime, are wonderful, and I have been granted numberless to witness. These late sunsets of September are the loveliest of all.

[176]

October

COUNTING, CALENDAR-WISE, THE FIRST DAY OF JANUARY AS the accepted New Year, I also note three more. One is not a fixed date: anytime when spring flowers, in any part of the hemisphere seems to me a beginning; but my emotional year starts with December twenty-fifth, and my personal year on the first day of October, my birthday.

So I feel more fortunate than most—four annual new-year celebrations, however they may differ!

I have already said I do not make January first resolutions. But this October I shall give myself a present, which is, perhaps, in the nature of a resolution or an endeavor. It is expressed in the words of Max Ehrmann, who wrote, "beyond a wholesome discipline, be gentle with yourself."

It is doubtful if self-scourging ever saved the soul. And while we are told to consider our mistakes, I don't think we were intended to hang them on the walls of our

[177]

minds like unpleasant pictures and spend our time looking
at them. I know people who do, and who, if a misfortune
occurs, immediately feel that it must be some form of punishment and hunt back in the attics of memory to find
out for what?

Mostly, they'll find that the law of justice operated
at the time. It doesn't have to strike twice unless one makes
the same mistake again.

Mistakes are acts from which you learn and, having
learned, go on. Looking back is not good unless, confronted
with a similar choice, you glance over your shoulder, remember you once made the wrong one, and then, make
the right. I have wasted more time fretting over things
which happened forty or fifty years ago, time I could have
put to very good use and in which I might have accomplished
something! Mistakes, once committed, need not be obstacles
and can be steppingstones. You don't walk backward on
steppingstones, I hope.

In our attempts to be patient with others, in the truly
sincere desire to understand and to fulfill our obligations
toward them—or our duty, if you prefer what is to me a
harder word—in our earnest wish to forgive them, we over-
look ourselves. It is unlikely that anyone sits down and
says, "I will be patient with myself, and understanding.
I will fulfill my obligations toward, and forgive, myself."

In Ecclesiastes it is written, "Love thine own soul,
and comfort thine heart."

People who hate themselves, and therefore their own
souls, find it difficult not to hate other people. Those who

cannot learn to comfort their own hearts can rarely comfort hearts of others.

If you regard your soul—or spirit—as part of God, created by Him and infused by Him with the Divine Immortal spark, it isn't hard to love it. The soul does not afflict your physical mind and body; your physical mind and body afflict the soul.

When we review our sins of commission and omission, we usually either criticize ourselves unmercifully or excuse ourselves—thus falling between two stools. The better way is to look at each day's flaws, whether created in ignorance or by choice, admit them and be sorry for them. And after that forget them; try not to stumble over the same rocks again, but smooth them into steppingstones and move forward.

Everything moves forward—seasons, time, people. Nothing truly living is static, and to regress is to end as an abandoned infant, in instability.

Somewhere in my family a delightful superstition arose years ago. I think it was my daughter, Hervey, who first heard it, and brought it home. On the first day of the month, if you desired good luck, you said when you woke, and before you said anything else, "Rabbit, Rabbit." Then upon arising, you walked backwards downstairs.

I used to try to remember, "Rabbit, Rabbit," but I don't believe I ever did. There was always something going on—children late for breakfast, zippers to be zipped, or a natural, "Good morning." Alas, poor Rabbit! As for walking downstairs backwards, I never attempted that. It's all I can do to get downstairs forwards. I have been afraid of stairs since childhood. So for me, I feel that walking downstairs backwards—oh, I have had to do it on ships' ladders but not on the first of the month—would not produce good luck, but a broken neck.

I think it charming of my mother to have borne me on October first—which was, according to my father, a beautiful, bright Sunday—and at eight o'clock in the morning, which is not too early and not too late. I am sure the trees were singing out in color in what was then the little town of New Rochelle, and I know we were close to the water. As my mother spent much of her time in my father's sailboat, prior to my birth, I have always insisted that there is more than the normal amount of salt in my blood. And I know that, when I was a child in Shelter Island and our land sloped to the water, I could wake almost any hour of the night and feel whether the tide was in or out, neap or flood.

Perhaps that is why I am unhappy if I am not somewhere near water—oh, not unhappy exactly, but restless. I would not be content on a mountain forever, although I love mountains, but when I am in a place which combines water with mountains, I am at peace.

Mountains are strength; mountains are beautiful in the shifting light, whether forested or bleak; mountains alter imperceptibly and with incredible slowness; the air about them is wonderful to breathe. Water is never still; it flows . . . pond or lake, river or brook, bay or ocean, always motion, however invisible in the little pools. There is always a stirring in the waters, and the irresistible headlong rush of brook to river and river to sea is marvellous to contemplate. In the oceans, tides and currents and cross-currents; in the rivers, eddies, whirlpools. . . . All water arrives at its destination, the sea . . . and under ocean currents, storm and disturbance, there is the unfathomable profundity, the deep deep quiet.

In one's personal landscape, there are also mountains to be climbed. The way is toilsome and dangerous . . . one slip, the fall, the painful getting up and starting again. There are drastic changes in temperature; there are valleys to look into and heights to look up to; rest places and then a going on again. Toward the top, the air is indescribably pure to breathe.

There's a mountain which is life-high, and there are daily mountains—all leading upward.

It is harder for the average man or woman to make the lifelong daily ascensions than for explorers to conquer Everest.

Then, too, there are swift water and slow, pools and backwaters, inlets and the bays, the brook which is easy to jump or wade, the body of water which is bitter cold, and the moment when you say, "I can't swim further."

Go with the tide and not against it. For the traveller on foot to the heights, for the swimmer moving toward the eternal sea, there is always the destination.

I like to go along . . . I like to go along with people, events and living. There have been many years in which I fought tides and currents, and slid down mountains, overpowered by avalanches. I didn't want to go along then. I wanted things my way. I wanted to get wherever I was going fast; find the short cuts, the easy ascents, the quiet pool—in which I preferred to stay. But, having, not without anguish, learned that the other way is, in the end, easier, I go along . . . not always perhaps, as there are times when it simply doesn't seem possible. . . . That's when you stick the pick in the ice of the mountain, or rest your oars in the little boat, or if you're swimming, somehow get to shore and just sit there. But sooner or later, you go on again.

I hope this is a year of going along for me, and that my present to myself, while not wrapped in bright paper or tied with big bows, will last me all year. As I pray that I may be kinder to those I meet, I shall ask to be kinder to myself. I'll go along with myself in that way, too.

We often hear the old expression that someone is "beside himself"—with rage, grief, frustration, or panic. I have often said that I am beside myself for one reason or another, and I find it an uncomfortable place to be!

I think it time to change the interpretation . . . to go along, beside oneself, companionably and in quiet, is probably what we were meant to do.

It is not often given us, except sometimes in dreams, to be two people, both of them ourselves, so one self may look at the other. My daughter dreamed the other night that she was in a sort of auditorium. She was also on the side lines looking at herself. Well, now and then during a lifetime there are moments when, for a split second, we do see ourselves from outside. Or is it from inside? Is it with the wiser vision of the spirit? Such moments are revealing but do not disclose what we would like to see, or what we thought, hoped, imagined and believed.

That is because, outside or in, we do not see the picture clear. I think I know myself. I am sure I know my good qualities and bad; I sometimes believe I understand my motivations. But I don't—really. And to see ourselves as others see us, as Robert Burns wished, would be an extraordinary experience, for no two people see anyone alike . . . in all relationships—parent, child, lover, friend, husband, wife, stranger . . . none sees the same thing. And what each sees in another today he may not see tomorrow. Only God sees in all dimensions, and whole.

"No one understands me," says a discontented woman. Does she *want* people to understand her? Can she understand herself?

It is not difficult to understand in general the outsides of people, so to speak . . . or to know, if you are anything of an amateur psychologist, what makes them tick. You can fit almost everyone into convenient pigeonholes . . . blame environment for this, a parent for that, a wife or husband or child for something else. You can dissect people according to your knowledge and in the light which your personal relationship with them has cast . . . here is vanity, here pride, there generosity, cruelty, or kindness . . . a hundred identifiable traits, each a strand with which the pattern appears to have been woven.

Basically we understand needs, we all have the same, so

know what others need. We know that, like us, they were born, and like us, must in the body die. We know that few— I've not met any—escape the sting of injustice; the lash of physical pain; the close, dark room of sorrow; the loneliness of fear. We know all this, yet still have not reached the essential person. No one does.

We can put people into categories. They don't quite fit. For every living human being in this world is absolutely unique. No two exactly alike, not even identical twins. . . . They may be, in outward appearance and often are in tastes, in tendencies toward this or that weakness, in the salient characteristics and reactions. But in each is a spirit which no one else on earth possesses, the mind which is not a replica of any other. . . . In every family, the interested can trace heredity factors: Susy is like her maternal grandmother; John resembles his father in looks, his mother in disposition; and I'm certain sister didn't get that temper from any of us; it must be from great grandfather Smith!

None in a family inherits precisely what the rest do; so each is different.

There are scientific words for all this. I can't spell any one of them but "genes," so I won't try. But while the coloration of youngest leaf on the family tree may resemble that of a leaf branches removed, and while it may be swayed by the same winds which trouble the topmost, it has its own life, beauty and irregularities.

To understand all is to forgive all, it is said. To forgive even *without* full understanding must be the true endeavor. For none understands all but our Creator.

Do you ever reread books which, years ago, you read with pleasure and excitement? I do. Before I moved from the other house, I had well over four thousand books. I had gone through them as best I could, and sorted them into categories. I sent many mystery books and novels to friends and hospitals, reference and nonfiction to the local library. I had reduced the number of volumes to about two thousand, which I thought this, the new house, could accommodate. It didn't, so after the move, I kept on sorting. The children had many books of their own from childhood through college; these I gradually persuaded them to take from shelves or the overflow in the attic. The rest I sent to the town in which we formerly lived where there was a thrift shop which helped support the Visiting Nurses' Association.

Finally, what remained were settled on shelves in library and living room. Then came a time when it was hard for me to read contemporary fiction, and night after night, I reread books which had been issued in the 'thirties. Many of them were English, which had never had American publication. I had, over the years, collected them through the English bookshop in New York, now defunct, but then operated by friends. Of the many books by each writer I had, when I moved, saved a few of each.

So, in a way, I returned to the past; not the far unknown, but the immediate past, and read a number of novels which at the time of publication had impressed me.

It was extraordinary how few, after approximately twenty years' time, held up.

Some were valid because they dealt with essentials, which are as true today as yesterday and will be as true tomorrow. Others were still enchanting, being in the realm of fantasy, which is timeless.

Some, which I read for the third or fourth time, emerged as period pieces. Their conceptions and tabus no longer exist, but they will be invaluable for the author who, writing twenty years from now, of a period of which he personally knows nothing, wishes to learn the thinking, speech, tabus and manners of its people. . . .

Recently I picked up a novel written by my cousin, Paul. He is now gone from here. Immeasurably gifted, and for the last years of his life, very ill, he wrote a number of books. This one was his longest and, I believe, the one upon which he expended the most time and thought. It was published in 1946.

Rereading, I was stunned by its hopelessness. It is the detailed, thoughtful story of four men who meet one another in the First World War, on submarine duty, on this side of the ocean. Diversified in background, education and circumstances, they encounter one another many years later. Painstakingly, my cousin traced each of their lives from its beginning. Nothing was omitted of the years between 1918 and the late 'thirties.

Yet, reading it again, after twelve years, it seems to me to echo only times, not timelessness. Paul chose hard, differing ways for his four carefully delineated principal characters. What happened to them was important to him. Yet none really emerges as forward-going or God-conscious. Not even the good men—and two are, as we understand the word, "good" on the surface—or the "good" women who come into the story.

I laid the book aside, proud of my cousin's gift and effort—his was a far greater gift than my own—and saddened by his "water-skiing." For, much as he tried to delve into man's thinking, below the outward circumstances of poverty or riches, belief or nonbelief, background and lack of it, he was not able profoundly to impart man's evolving spirit. I daresay he knows now. Yet the book is a good book. Twelve years after publication, it may be, as a critic would say, "dated," but now and then there emerges something not dated, a validity apart from devised plot or situation.

How well-nigh impossible it is, in any area, truly to write of man! Except for a handful of geniuses who could, in their time, write what would remain valid, whenever it was read. That is why Shakespeare has survived the centuries. He wrote of his times, using other men's plots; he intended his plays to be seen, not read; but in each there are people who move, in whatever costume, modes or manners, and who are, today, as real as when created. Few writers achieve this; they write of, and for, their own era only.

As a so-called popular writer I have produced many books which, in whatever shallow fashion, reflected the times. I recall, not long ago, that my daughter-in-law, Janet, chancing upon an old book of mine, took it upstairs and read it. She came down, with her eyes laughing. "Did men really *ever*

wear dancing pumps, and did girls rouge their kneecaps?"
she inquired. And I answered, "I've forgotten, but if I said
so, then they did. I wrote it as it was at the time."

I have a warm feeling for novelists, whatever their era.
We read them now, those whose talent has weathered the
years, though young people who cannot recall even the First
World War and the times which followed are incredu-
lous.

If I were now writing a period novel—I've done several
in days past—I would do my research factually, through the
many books which list events and changes, and even the
widely read books, successful plays and discussed theories
of the times. But I would also find, at the library, the fiction
which tells what the barriers and tabus were, how people
spoke and thought, how they dressed and amused themselves,
what they ate and what they sang.

If this present civilization perishes and if, centuries
hereafter, new generations excavate the ruins, they may discover a number of things, including books, which have not
been destroyed by time, bombing, floods and earthquakes.
Those of the geniuses—if this period has produced any—
they will readily understand, as the stuff of life is basic, and
who writes about it follows his ancestors and anticipates his
descendants. What is basic in life? Basic are the needs:
shelter, nourishment, love; and the reaching up to God . . .
by whatever name He is called in whatever generation and
century. Basic are death, hunger, confusion and struggle.
Happiness is basic, and simple joy. This, if now we write
about it, will be comprehended by those who read centuries

later—if, indeed, any language now extant can still be read. But, provided they desire to reconstruct past ages for their own educational and historical purposes, they will turn to those surviving books of writers contemporaneous with those times. These will tell in fiction and in nonfiction, how people outwardly lived. For this is history neatly set down at the very moment it was made.

Time is like feminine dress. There are classic patterns, falling into classic shapes, which never go out of style. Some years ago the designer, Elizabeth Hawes, wrote a book called *Fashion Is Spinach*. And she was so right.

Fashion in clothes—men's, women's, children's—alters. None, of course, as radically as women's. I have costume books which show clothes from the earliest times, and some which depict clothing, male and female, together with accessories, and colors, from the early sixteen hundreds through the nineteen-forties. Look at these books. Sooner or later everything returns, if modified or exaggerated. And every season fashion changes: short hemlines, long hemlines, close-fitting waists, no waists.

I recall the frightening fashions prior to the First World War, immediately afterwards, and in the 'twenties. I remember my wedding dress. I thought it charming. Of ivory-tinted satin, it ended just below the knees. And to this was added a seven-foot train!

The wedding dresses of my mother's period were by my day completely out of fashion: long-sleeved, high-necked, demure and with hemlines which flowed into the train—if any. I have seen these return, adopted. As of now, I have not seen my treasured nineteen-twenty atrocity come back. I hope I never shall but, I daresay, I must.

A dear friend of mine, raised in the opulent era, has in her wardrobes beautiful evening dresses created for her mother by great Paris dressmakers. They literally stand alone because of the weight and durability of the materials, the like of which we do not see nowadays. Sometimes Rita alters them to suit her own figure and wears them to formal affairs. She also owns an evening cloak made for her grandmother, as unaffected by time as any work of art. Occasionally she wears that, too. She knows that sooner or later fashions return.

No designer can ring all the changes indefinitely; one season we have an Asian influence, another the Balkan. Anxiously, the great dressmakers consult with one another. "Short or long?" they ask. "Shall we put them in potato sacks, or constrict the waist?" They go to museums and look at the Grecian and Egyptian, the Byzantine, the Persian, and adapt these. There is a flurry of South Seas Fashions, of Indian saris. Chinese motifs appear.

But that is fashion, and few women are equipped with income and figure to follow it. For in a season, it is over and the designers decide to reverse themselves.

The average woman who cannot afford vagaries, or discard a frock worn only once or twice, contents herself with what is becoming; the hem length which suits her, the lines which enhance her, the clothes which make her prettier, not grotesque. Only a woman not endowed by nature with attraction can afford the expense which draws eyes to what she wears, not to herself.

My father used to look at my mother's hats with horror. Most of them, if bought at ultra-fashionable shops, he would insist that she return. He had a criterion. "A woman's hat" he used to say "should frame her face; it should draw attention to her features not to the hat."

He, like Elizabeth Hawes, was right.

I remember some of the hats I wore in my youth. I remember the cloches. I recall a hat like an inverted wastebasket, lavishly trimmed with bright red cherries, drooping on their stems. I had, at one time, a picture of myself in a black net dress, which displayed a waist measuring eighteen scant inches. This might be something to hand down to my grandchildren who, because of proper feeding and supplementary diet, will probably grow into giants. But alas, in the photograph I am wearing an enormous hat, with white ostrich plumes. My small-boned face is lost. It looks like a peanut which, by a freak of nature, has grown on a palm tree. I am convinced that no woman should ever have a photograph taken in a hat!

I often heard my lawyer father judicially remark that, of all women's clothing, the garment worn by trained nurses was the most beautiful. And that, mind you, in an era when they had never heard of nylon, but rustled starchily about beds and corridors. Hemlines were long, as were sleeves; collars were high, yet he said, "There is nothing to compare with a nurse's uniform, which transforms a plain woman into a lovely one, a lovely woman into a beauty, and a beauty into an angel."

If, as I, you have lived, by October first, sixty-five full

years, you have seen many fashions come and go, not only in women's dress, but also in men's. You will have seen what was once accepted become tabu and what was once tabu become routine.

There have been fashions in furniture as well. . . . I remember bead curtains and gilded pampas grass in equally gilded lengths of pipe. I recall "Oriental" dens, with crossed swords, silvered shields, bright cushions on the sofa and mother-of-pearl inlaid taborets. I remember Morris chairs. . . .

Now the fad is antiques (once flung into basements, barns or attics), or the modern furniture which becomes almost anything you ask of it. I am a little afraid to sit on the chairs which rise from stems and offer scoops for my comfort. But I understand they are wonderful.

I remember the telephones upon the walls and those upright instruments upon desk or hall table; those which were lateral, like, yet unlike, the early Continental ones. And now I dial mine and it can be bought in colors to match all rooms.

Just as there have been changing fashions in everything we use, wear and eat (Have you ever been served rattlesnake meat, before dinner? I have, and nearly perished when I found out, yet I hear that fried locusts are now quite in the mode), just as there are fashions in schools (which rise and fall with tides in education), thinking, and in everything you see and hear, so there are fashions in religion—modern schools of thought, theological or otherwise, and modern approaches to the mysteries of man's spirit and God's existence.

But the belief that God does exist can never go out of fashion, for He is more basic than the need for shelter or even human love. He waits, and does not alter. It is to Him, however crushed by the pressures of haste and today's living, that we must turn. We must. For a universe without Him is unthinkable.

"This too will pass," we learn to say of our outward distress and anxiety. Everything will pass—today, tomorrow and the day after tomorrow. What we think and feel and believe we know will, at least in part, be discarded by the next generation. Has not every generation discarded as impractical or too idealistic the beliefs of the former?

But God will not pass away; or the aspirations of the most confused human spirit toward Him.

Every life is a moment in His time. It may be fifty, sixty or eighty years, as we count it; it may even be a century. It is still but a moment to Him. It is, as we live it, vitally important to us. It is not to Him. We are important—not the time in which we live but ourselves, and the use we make of our time.

So now it is October, and I wish, for whoever reads, many happy returns of my recent birthday.

TWELVE

November

LONG BEFORE THE SEASON WE CALL THANKSGIVING, I WILL
have decorated the house outside and in, with symbols of
autumn and harvest.

From Cape Cod I shall have brought home the gray
pearls of the bayberry, clustered along their black branches,
and put them in bowls and Chinese wall vases; and bought
from wayside stands bittersweet, orange-red; and the dried
flowers—I do not know what they are called—which are as
yellow as dandelions. In a blue bowl and pitcher, they create
a blaze, like sunlight, when the room dims with dusk. I like
to use ornamental gourds in the entry hall, heaped in a
celadon bowl . . . the small ones, round as miniature oranges
or shaped like lemons, green-striped, rosy or yellow, dark
jade, white. Last season a friend gave me some from her
own garden, and they were doubly welcome.

Outside, on the doorstep, I set pumpkins, not carved

into faces but unadorned; and I hang above the doorway many colored ears of corn. The most recent pumpkins met an untimely fate, for during one night some hungry small animal had eaten quite a wedge from each. Gussie, who officiates evenings, in my kitchen, inquired, could she have the pumpkins? She could. She took them home, cut away the unsightly parts, and returned to me in triumph with a delicious pumpkin pudding.

That was better than one season during which I forgot my pumpkins until, on a warm day, toward spring, I lifted one by its stem and afterward, with broom and water, scrubbed the stones of the terrace which were lavishly splashed.

The gourds, as time goes on, grow as light as air; the colors fade, but I leave them where they are until spring.

As Thanksgiving nears, it occurs to me that it is unthankful to be grateful only at a certain time of year, set aside by Proclamation.

Thinking back over the past twelve months, I find that, as in all years, I have more for which to be grateful than to deplore. I have throughout my entire life received more good than evil, made more friends than enemies, been given more love than indifference, more kindness than cruelty.

Those who spend their time unhappily recounting their "ill luck" and the terrible things which "happened" to them are unfortunate beyond their own imagining, because they do not pause in the recital of their miseries to consider, and be grateful for, the good. Everyone has good bestowed upon him . . . first of all, life.

But, people ask, "What good has life brought *me?*"

The answer is also a question: *"What good have you brought to life?"* For life gives sentience, consciousness, if nothing else. How you use it determines the good life can, and will, bring.

No matter how difficult this existence—and I know how hard it can be—it is living, here and now, in preparation for a larger life at some future, unguessed date. No matter how many the problems and hardships, we are, in this world, alive. We breathe the air and see the sky. The sun, the stars, the vast stretches of the sea, the little enclosure of a pond, the wide reaches of a lake belong to us all. Trees are ours and the flowers in the field, even if on property we do not own. But people rarely regard these gifts as special. They groan their way to bed at night, then groan themselves upright in the morning.

Most of us have problems relating to health or finances, or anxieties over people we love. We are so preoccupied with worry, pain or unhappiness that we cannot find anything for which we feel we can be thankful. But cannot we be grateful that we are sufficiently alive to feel whatever may trouble us?

I have learned over a period of time to be almost unconsciously grateful—as a child is—for a sunny day, blue water, flowers in a vase, a tree turning red. I have learned to be glad at dawn and when the sky is dark. Only children and a few spiritually evolved people are born to feel gratitude as naturally as they breathe, without even thinking. Most of us come to it step by painful step, to discover that gratitude is a form of acceptance.

For each lesson learned, there is reward. As children in kindergarten are given a book into which they paste a symbol of a morning well spent, every adult day can achieve its commendation. I don't know what the ultimate reward is; awareness of the completed task is reward enough for now.

Last summer I sometimes rose to the early light; sometimes overslept until the sun shone, or the rain fell straight, or the fog came creeping in. Just to rise and look at the still cove or the further ocean was enough; to smell coffee, to sit at a table and look toward a curve of hills, a bend of beach and the gulls flying over water, was something at which to wonder and for which to be grateful, although it happened day after lovely day.

Most of us forget to take time for wonder, praise and gratitude until it is almost too late.

Gratitude is a many-colored quality, reaching in all directions. It goes out for small things and for large; it is a Godward going.

The so-called great events bespeak gratitude—the dollars dropped in our laps, the unexpected awards, acclaim, the sudden light which penetrates a darkness of despair. All of us have known these larger moments, and most of us are grateful. But I think we should daily remember the small and the routine things, which call for a gratitude we rarely express and often do not even recognize.

We forget to be thankful for the basic things, those

[197]

which each man and woman expects as a birthright: love, which is emotional security; food and shelter, however unexciting (but who can live in two houses at once or eat more than three meals a day?); friends; understanding, and God's bright world about us day after day.

I enjoy feeling gratitude but don't compel myself to remember it every November. I don't deliberately remember it at all. It comes, on a winter's day or spring evening, in the dawn of a summer morning or the sunset of the autumn. It comes at any hour, at any time. It is as simple as that. It brings with it no crushing sense of duty, no feeling of obligation.

Since last Thanksgiving I have had major things for which to give thanks. I have seen another grandchild enter this life. I have experienced long days of anxiety over the physical illnesses of my children and watched light emerge from what seemed darkness. I have been agonized over problems in my immediate family, only to witness their slow but steady progression toward solutions.

But I am also thankful for the things which, by comparison, are lesser: for daily communications with those I love and who love me; for food and shelter; for awareness of all beauty, whether it be a heart-stirring manifestation or a small weed at the roadside's edge.

I have managed to return to the road which for many years I travelled in my particular task of creative writing. For this renewal of effort I am grateful.

I think at Thanksgiving we tend to remember—if anything—the larger benevolences. The usual pictures come to us of Pilgrim fathers, laden tables and people gathered around them. But why on one day only? Just as it seems customary for the Christmas spirit to endure but for a day or a week, it seems normal to most of us to admit that we are thankful on one day set aside by our President. Why not every day? Every day we—even the most unhappy, ill-adjusted and self-pitying among us—have something for which to be grateful. We have, except for the very few, some form of love. We have, in varying degrees, nourishment, light, air and shelter.

I remember an old hymn that amazed me, as a child, because it seemed so solemn and conjured up fantastic pictures. And when I grew older I thought the phrasing extravagant: "Where every prospect pleases and only man is vile." Every prospect does not please, but if you consider it with the eyes of understanding, you come to the realization that the world God shaped in Creative Intelligence is beautiful. Even the wasteland and desolate, bare mountains have beauty; in form and shifting color God's earthly universe is all beauty. Where there is ugliness in city slum, in lands deliberately denuded of trees, in the repeated patterns of houses too close together, man has made it so.

The Gospels tell us, "God so loved the world." He does, I know, all parts of it, however we regard them. And all human beings in the world, whatever their condition of life and development. I do not believe that one human soul is more important to Him than another. Some are further advanced in thinking and in service to humanity than others— a woman like Helen Keller, a man like Albert Schweitzer, and others who in stupendous human endeavor, understanding and love for their fellow men are valuable to humanity. Any good man or woman, however obscure, is also more valuable to the world than those we call evil. Yet, as souls, no more important to the Creator.

I have never met a parent of a deficient, handicapped child who loved that child less than the healthy, intelligent children in the family.

Usually, such a child has a harder path than brother or sister; it learns, if at all, far less and with great difficulty. One small act of recognition or awareness is therefore a greater accomplishment than the normal, forward-going behavior of the normal child, and the parents are accordingly grateful.

So, in a larger way, must God be grateful when one of His creations knows a stirring of the spirit and learns haltingly to read in the book of law, and to turn a page. This has been called salvation. Call it what you will. I believe that souls are saved; I also believe that none is ever lost if the desire to go forward is even dimly felt.

Remember the ninety and nine?

I am grateful for this world, and for all that I see and hear in it, although I often see and hear things which are unpleasant. I am grateful that I *can* see and hear.

When at mealtime, I say Grace silently or aloud, giving thanks and asking for my daily bread, it does not transmute coffee, fruit and toast into something unexpected. The fruit is as it was grown, the coffee as I made it, good or bad, the toast dark or light, but there is a special refreshment in the food over which one has said words of gratitude.

Gratitude is not obligation. To be under obligation is to live with a burden. Most of us hate it. But to be grateful is, in its own way, a living joy. Gratitude springs unbidden from the very essence of the heart and spirit.

I *like* being grateful. I like being grateful to those closest to me for love and kindness and consideration. I *like* being grateful to God for friends, for everything with which He so bountifully endows me, whether or not I deserve it. I don't think we have always to deserve. We don't give only to the deserving. If we are giving persons, we give to all who need.

The natural and material gifts which reach us are not hard to tabulate; each can make his own list. The gifts of love, sacrifice and devotion come readily to mind; and the benevolence accorded us through nature's bounty—a mourning dove just flew past my window, the cardinals are in the feeder. There are also gifts given us by strangers, through their creative work, whether in the pages of a book, on a stage, in a concert hall, or through a painting which hangs on our walls, on those of friends, or in a museum.

Rarely, however, do we stop seriously to consider the spiritual gifts past answered prayer. Of this, we do think. But there is yet more.

Spiritual law bestows treasure past all calculation—and equally upon rich and poor, hungry and fed, happy and miserable, ill and well. The law, being love in principle and from the Source, must bestow.

I have spoken at length of love and of quietude but not much of spiritual joy. It is hard to express in the speech we use; it is difficult to formulate even in thought. I earnestly

believe that we are born with it, and the unreasoning child
will accept it as something which comes and goes, unidenti-
fied with anything outward; no reward, no present, no per-
mission to do something, not even his mother's arms and
his father's strength are the reasons for it; not the wind in
his hair nor the sense of running free in the sun. It wells
up within him, pure and nameless. Occasionally, as adults,
we also feel it, but usually look for a reason, endeavor to
attach it to something or someone—an achievement made,
an anxiety over, an unexpected, outward pleasure. But it
remains truly anonymous, dying once the pin of reason is
thrust through the bright luminous wings.

I can tell you something of what spiritual joy is not.
It is not happiness, or pleasure. It is not satisfaction. It has
nothing to do with our circumstances, states of health, or
material security.

Born in, and of, the spirit, it is unaffected by whatever
takes place outside of us, and within the physical mind. It
is not slain by sorrow, by loss, by resentment or frustration.
It lives, whether we know it or not, always and forever.

Usually, it cannot reach through to the physical intelligence because of what events and environment, hardships,
griefs and distresses have done to the mind and, often, to
the body. But it is still there. If you buy a fine perfume, you
know that it has an essence, the basic ingredient. Spiritual
joy is like that—an essence; the core, woven in the very fabric
of the spirit.

I have sometimes been happy all day for several days
hand running. Yet, whatever there was in my situation which

did not seem good to me had in no way altered; it was perhaps not worse, but it wasn't better. Yet this joy remained, completely apart from anything I said, did, or outwardly felt.

Spiritual joy is a Law, which operates whether or not we are aware of it; and for this joy there should be gratitude. Even a man without sight can be grateful for the flowers nearby or the arched sky above him. He cannot see them, yet he knows they are there.

Faith is another Law and if we possess it, there, too, is a gift. Belief is perhaps acquired, generally by example, education and our own hard work. But "Faith," said St. Paul, "is the substance of things hoped for, the evidence of things not seen."

Belief can be shattered; belief is, I hold, of the mind, heart and memory. It can be overthrown by an event or succession of events, questioned, pinpointed, discarded. "Religion," Marx said, "is the opium of the people." Opiates lull, and are often cut off. Belief sometimes operates as an opiate. With belief, you walk warily. These are not just phrases. I know what I am talking about. I have seen a cherished, accepted, if not profoundly examined, belief in a million fragments at my feet; bits of bright, beautiful, vulnerable stuff which could not be put together again.

Faith, which is of the spirit, is unshatterable. In Faith, trust is implicit. It is a law, and when everything has failed, and the belief which was classified and annotated has vanished, something of Faith remains. It is there, and immutable. It may not seem to be Faith in God. It may appear to be faith in a person or persons, in yourself, in your own ability to pull out of the quicksand. But it cannot be wholly eradicated, and *is* Faith in God, even as you deny Him.

Belief is wonderful if it sustains and is unshaken. But it is not always dependable. Faith is eternal, as is hope, because as human beings we must hope. Today is dreadful. Tomorrow will be better.

Knowledge is also firmer than any rock. Who has Faith, even if he does not recognize it, has also knowledge.

For these, be grateful. It is better to hold fast to one fragment of a true principle than slackly to grasp at a hundred differing aspects of it, and have true knowledge of nothing.

There is a road; it is straight and has been called narrow; it is not always level. From it, many paths lead away, and back again. Numberless people seek the road and, finding it, are attracted by the byways, return, move on for a time, and stray again.

It is the longer way 'round, really, but eventually most find themselves again, for the duration, upon the straight road. It leads down hill and up; it crosses rough places and sometimes there is darkness. But it never ends in confusion. The bypaths may conflict, and people run to and fro on this one and that, feeling it will be shorter and the goal nearer, for the short cut.

There are no short cuts.

By whatever name the road is called, let us be grateful for it. This road is never lonely; there is always the Companion.

People go shopping for beliefs as they do for groceries,

going from one supermarket to another; here there is more for your spiritual money; there you are given coupons of value; in this place, there is a two-for-one sale and in another fresher offerings, or shelves of delicacies more sustaining, more health-giving, according to the labels, or more exotic.

Some of these shops are on the bypaths and shoppers linger there. Yet, once you have found it, one road is best; the deviations can be disturbing.

No one receives all he desires from living. We are like children with our faces pressed against the windows of a pastry shop. So many desirable things! Have we enough to buy them? Can we afford this one or that? One, two or several? Must we then, regretfully, let the others go?

The answer is, yes.

Few, even the most fortunate, achieve all they dream, all they plan and pledge to accomplish. The child who has managed high school desires the university. The university graduate wants another degree or, having a good position, a better one. He may not get it, so he will always look back wondering where he failed or where someone else failed him.

The creative artist, the craftsman, never achieves his goal . . . if he has popularity he wants prestige; if he has prestige he yearns for popularity as well. If he has both, he longs for something beyond each.

There are seemingly humbler goals; a woman can believe her world would be complete if something extra were added: more salary for the breadwinner, a larger house, a finer neighborhood, task-relieving appliances.

There are those who aspire to the fundamentals of personal satisfaction: a compatible family life, a loving child, a child who will not only gladden them but astonish the world. Those whose children have deeply disappointed, even irradicably wounded them, will envy the parents of a good, plodding child.

We pick up a paper . . . here is a man with everything we do not have, high position, a great deal of money, a seemingly happy family. Yet he has committed suicide. Why? "He had everything to live for," we say to one another, astonished.

What?

"Well," we answer, "he had family, money—he could do anything, travel anywhere, maintain great houses, achieve positions of trust in government, society, finance."

What do we know of him or anyone? How can we guess at unfulfilled ambition or desire, the darkness overcoming the mind? What do we know of his pride or inner misery? His publicized fortune seems enormous to us, and even if he had lost three quarters of it, what was left would sustain us comfortably for the rest of our lives, but would it have sustained him?

And, finally, how do we know what we would have done in his place? Maybe once he believed in something, God, happiness, ambitions fulfilled, himself. But perhaps belief was too strongly centered in himself and when that went, everything did.

Tonight I was talking to a close friend about a situation in her family, and she said, "Maybe it's a blessing in disguise."

That is an old saying. It is one that many people laugh at as a cliché. But it can be truth itself.

Visualize a woman who has bought a house, having managed to save a little and move from a rented apartment. As are most houses, it was purchased with a mortgage lashed to it. This disturbs her. She hates the mortgage as if it were a deadly personal enemy. Yet, for the first time in her life, she is saving money; she has to, in order to meet the interest. She does so regularly; she has an equity in her house; she has a place in her community; she is, as the banks say, a good risk. That which she considers a millstone about her neck is really a blessing . . . in disguise.

There is a man who had, suddenly, an illness. His family after his return from the hospital put all their intelligence to bear on the things which would make him well; particularly they were aware of all that, to heal him, would have to be withheld. Later, when he had recovered, his work took him to a different state. He was well, he was fine, he was also on his own. His original trouble had been eradicated and did not return, so, although he had been warned to lose weight and had done so, he proceeded happily to regain it. He found himself presently in another hospital, not with the illness of the preceding year but with what was apparently an overstrained heart. Perhaps this, too, is a blessing in disguise, and from now on he will be careful.

Sometimes the blessings are so well disguised that we do not see beneath the mask until months, even years thereafter.

Are you a step-retracer? I am, and this peculiar quality is not exclusively a feminine trait. Physically, I retrace so many steps that, laid end to end, they would carry me, in a day's time, downtown and back. Turn me loose in a kitchen and I run between pots and pans, sink, range and refrigerator. I carry things endlessly, being too impatient to put them on the tray which would save the steps. I never go to bed and stay there. I am up and down. I have left one pair of glasses downstairs or forgotten to turn out the outside lights. I didn't bring up the book I'd laid aside to read in bed. I have mislaid the TV program. I was certain I had taken everything upstairs with me but, no, there are at least three things I am sure I can't live without during the night. And I always forget to take a handkerchief from pocket, purse or drawer.

It's a tiring thing, retracing steps.

I suppose one reason I do this is that I think of other things, and never see what is in front of me. I can leave a room six times and go back—often because of pure laziness. In order to turn on the lights which flood the enclosed stairway I have only to go into the entry hall and touch a switch. But to do that, I must cross the study and living room. So, I turn out the study lights and creep upstairs in the dark. I am always losing my way and crashing into doorways, mantelpieces and the like. Once in the upper hall, I turn the lights on, but by that time I am battered and bruised.

The other night I managed to take everything up with me: a fur coat, a hat, a handbag and a tall glass of orange juice. I saved myself steps by putting on the hat and the coat for the brief journey, but I didn't turn on the light.

Just try going up thirteen steps in pitch-darkness with a glass of orange juice in one hand!

Introspection can be overdone. But sometimes it is wise to retrace the steps of your life, which have brought you to where you are now—to see why you took so many steps in the first place . . . why you went back again and again . . . and why you didn't turn on the lights when all it would have cost you was a little effort.

Now, as I look at the clock, measuring the distance to the entry hall and the light switch, and look unhappily at what passes for typewritten pages, I am struck with the logical thought that, before I go upstairs, I must retrace my mental steps. I must go back to November and Thanksgiving which set me to writing and thinking of gratitude . . . thankfulness for spiritual joy, for faith, for the direct road, for the blessing in disguise. And even for the ability to laugh at myself when I consider all my unnecessary steps. No efficiency engineer would tolerate me and my lack of method.

So November goes quietly or stormily into the Christmas month, which I love, whatever it brings in weather, and there is another blessing; another December for giving and loving and rejoicing, and for knowing that Thanksgiving is for always.

Retracing the mental steps I know that much has been given me since last Thanksgiving, and some things, denied. And I think I've learned how a Thanksgiving prayer should be fashioned. I've said it before, but here it is again:

"Thank You, Father," I would say, "for all You have given me, are giving and will give; and also for all that has been withheld, for if You withhold, then I know it is best for me."

It takes quite a spell of living to learn to be thankful for the things you haven't had, even though you may have prayed for them, but your Father in Heaven knows your needs.

❧ THIRTEEN

December

As the year, for me, began with December, how can it better end? December weather, this year, is as chancy as last, given to fits of rain and starts of snow, yet sometimes offering, as if in apology, a day tinged with the colors of a distant spring. As always, this month affords at least three weeks of commotion. For some, the confusion began much further back . . . perhaps even late last summer. It centered around questions: What shall we give to whom? With which child, or children, spend the holidays? How many will be with us?

There is also the problem of money: We can't afford this. We shouldn't buy that. We must, even when we can't, for you know how much *they* spend!

The pre-Christmas turmoil, harried and material, is often, as a friend of mine remarked, "enough to drive you out of your mind." But let us stop and consider: Who, at the same time, are we driving out of theirs?

Many profess to ignore, forget, shrug off or hate the season. It is, they argue, wholly commercial. They do not pause to think of the merchant, in his private uncertainty: Has he overstocked? Which item will sell? Which will not? He has to be commercial, for he must earn his daily bread. Everyone who has anything to sell, whether goods or personal services, must consider commerce, even though certain services seem to be of loftier quality than others.

It is true that nowadays Christmas decorations make their appearance so far in advance that, by the time the Eve comes, we regard them with a jaundiced eye. In recent years, people appear to have sat up nights, inventing bigger and gaudier attention-getting fantasies. There is apparent a certain rivalry. More roofs are laden with reindeer than ever before, and it would seem that if Harry attaches the conventional eight to the sleigh, his next-door neighbor must have ten. Multicolored lights are not new, on either indoor or outdoor trees, but now we have a surfeit of lights on a plethora of trees—I have counted as many as six around one house—and green and red bulbs flash on and off around doorways, looking rather seagoing, port and starboard, while lights writhe around eaves, and drip down, in color.

Santa Claus is not Christmas.

Santa should be a symbol of tender gaiety, past the material giving. He represents material giving, of course; sometimes grudgingly, often from a curious sense of duty; but, at best, frequently with sacrifice and, in the majority of cases, with love. For love, if not originally present is often engendered by the act of giving.

Look beneath the tinsel for the treasure.

The Christian world celebrates and, when it stops to remember what it is celebrating, is the better for it. A large portion of the non-Christian world, conforming to friends and neighbors, celebrates Santa Claus, and even trims trees, which were not, in origin, Christian at all. And many people who worship at other altars are sensitive to the joy and gratitude which is the essence of this season. Remember when, on the borders of hostile lands, non-Christian soldiers of the United Nations Forces took over sentry duty in order that their Christian brothers might worship at ancient shrines?

Christmas is a Baby and His parents. Christmas is a promise. It is looking back into times gone by and forward into days to come.

Christmas is in the unexpected gift: flowers from an acquaintance; a telephone call from someone you haven't heard from in years, and who, you thought, had forgotten you; it is in a card from overseas, a letter from a stranger, and a clumsily wrapped, handmade atrocity, fashioned by a child who has labored long, and with sticky hands.

None of this is basically material.

Christmas is an urge to give, to do, to be. It may last a very short time—and usually does—but, during it, the human spirit attains a fractional growth.

Many Bible students dispute the date of Jesus' birth. It was not, they say, December twenty-fifth; some believe it closer to three months later.

Dates are unimportant.

Others question the stable. Almost twice a thousand

years have come and gone and, through hundreds of them, men have read, written, argued and debated what took place on what we call Christmas Eve.

To me, in the Gospel according to St. Luke, there are ten tragic words and these are ". . . because there was no room for them in the inn."

For almost two thousand years there has still been no room at the inn for humility and gentleness, compassion and love, for revelation and wonder.

This visible world is composed of nations; nations of communities; communities of people. None but the most innocent among us expects mass spiritual awakening, in or out of any religion or creed—not any more. Most of us instinctively know that awakening begins in the individual.

Because in the inn of the world there has been no room, the world is outraged, knows unease and terror; people fight and kill, endure wars, experience horror, build concentration camps and set neighbor against neighbor. Countries perish; their people vanish from the face of the patient earth. Because there is no room at the inn, there are children desolate, women weeping, men lying faceless beneath the sky.

It is in the individual human spirit that the door of the inn must open wide in welcome, and so remain. For it is only through the human heart and understanding, and the knowledge of the Spiritual Law, ordained for all people, no matter where the accident of birth has placed them, or what creed they embrace, that the Christ-consciousness can enter in.

Not long ago a stranger wrote me, whether with or without approval, I cannot tell, that in my nonfiction writing I am "very personal."

Perhaps; and if so, it is because I have never been able to understand or deal with abstractions; so I can only set down what I have learned to believe and what I believe I have learned. The more we learn, the more there is to know. Before we are equipped to write the simplest sentence, we must master the alphabet. I am convinced that our lives, however long or short, are well spent in learning the ABCs of living, and that trying to skip grades is futile. There are no Phi Beta Kappas in kindergarten, and we have a great deal of time in which to go on to a higher education. We have Eternity.

Wherever we live, whatever our work, whoever we meet, individual spheres of influence are wider than we realize. A casual word to a friend may affect the life of a stranger; an attitude, kind and compassionate, harsh and biased, will affect many lives, known and unknown to us. It is a responsibility to be placed in this kindergarten we call "living." Each of us, whether conscious of it or not, is either a channel through which great spiritual forces may flow or one almost wholly sealed against them.

There are people who say—and not always because of grief or frustration—that they would like to leave the kindergarten. Because they envision the golden streets and responsive harps of a pictorial teaching? I do not know. But at some moment of valid desperation almost all of us have wished to leave.

Hung-Wu, who lived a long time ago, said that the

house of life has many windows. In this house, each has his personal room. I realize that I must become familiar and friendly with my personal room, as I must live in it. Sometimes it seems very cramped—the walls close in, the ceiling descends; sometimes it is airless, and windows which afforded agreeable outlooks give suddenly upon misery. Then, I wish to push out the walls, push up the ceiling, and shatter —or shutter—the windows. Sometimes the room has been wholly without light. But live in it I must, and I had best make alterations in it: change the décor, knock out a partition or two, move the furniture about, fashion wider windows—and look from each.

If I am to be comfortable in this room, wherein for a certain number of years I am to dwell, I must warm it with love, cool it with quietude, cushion it with compassion and leave the door unlocked for friend or stranger. I must do all within my capacity to make my room livable, set a stamp of individuality upon it, keep it in order, and inform it with a little beauty, before I am asked to move away.

I must know, when the dark comes in, where the light switch is. I must illumine my room with trust.

I have learned, now, not to be uncomfortable in it, not lonely. I am not afraid of this room. I shall not be afraid of the next.

The idea that it is desirable to move is generally projected because so many of us think that a departure solves everything. It doesn't. When you get on a plane, or train, or ship to go somewhere—actively disliking, or bored by, the place you leave—you believe that the point of arrival will

be more attractive. Do not delude yourself. You take yourself with you on your trip. The desire to escape from whatever burdens assail us is integral to all. But most of us know
that we do not leave these behind us when we depart—for
any place—for they are within us; we do not escape ourselves.

Let us be happy, each in his own room. None has oc-
cupied his room before; nor will again. Each is unique.

Now that Christmas is here and we decorate the rooms
of the houses in which we live, let each also decorate his
personal living room with the color of joy. And build in
each a shrine, for a room without worship is bare and com-
fortless. Worship is love, love is a Law, and the Law is God.

In your room, in mine, in everyone's, God is watcher,
listener and guest. He is companion, tenant and landlord.
None in his room is ever alone.

Let me write down for you a little verse which purports
to be an old Arabian song. I chanced upon it tonight as
I sat reading over after-dinner coffee, the inside wooden
blinds closed, while through some of the narrow, open
shutters the starlight streamed. There are garnet roses all
about and, in bowls of dark glass, the red berries and edged
leaves of holly. Everywhere the Christmas angels soar from
lintels and doorways. But, as yet, the tree is not in place.

I am in place, I am home. I am home in my house of
wood and in my house of flesh. I am home in my room in
the house of life. Though over the years, it has undergone
many changes, it is far from being all I wish it to be. But,
briefly, it is mine.

The verse is in a novel by an English woman who called

herself Richard Dehan. I believe her real name was Clothilde
Graves. The book, published in 1912, was, I think, my mother's. It is a long, detailed and impassioned tale, which has
much to do with the Crimean War. I do not know if the
verse is a true translation, or even if it is a translation at all.
Here it is:

"Thy Fate in the Balance; thy foot in the stirrup, before
thee the path of Honor. Ride on! Who knows what lies at the
end of the long journey? Ride on!

"Life and Love, Death and Sleep, these are from the Hand
of the Giver. Ride on! Thy Fate in the balance, thy foot in the
stirrup, before thee the path of Honor. Ride on!"

Save for the carols we love, can I give you a better song
to remember on a December night, as we approach the new
year?

In Conclusion . . .
IST CORINTHIANS 15:44

Under a warm September sky
    I saw a stirring in a tree,
And then, the trembling bird who looked
    From hill to sky, from sky to sea.

I marked him waver, watched him rise,
    Unsure, directionless, to fly
A little distance, or a great;
    The tree was still. The tree was I.

Rooted, and firm, and tolerant
    Of time and space and outward things,
Conforming to the troubled air,
    And insecurity on wings.

I am the tree; the roots unstirred.
I also am the pausing bird.